PRAISE FOR PREPARE FOR LEADERSHIP

"*Prepare For Leadership* is a must read! The book will inspire you to live a life of significance, and it will also give you wisdom years ahead of your age. I highly recommend that you read this leadership book no matter if you are a leader, or aspire to become one. I worked in the same company during the early 1980s with the author, Nile Ramsbottom, and he is a remarkable servant leader. We can all learn from his wisdom!"

—Mark Whitacre, coauthor of *Against All Odds*; subject of the blockbuster Warner Bros. movie *The Informant* (starring Matt Damon; directed by Steven Soderbergh)

"I recommend *Prepare for Leadership* not only as a good read, but as an excellent journey to be taken by anyone who approaches life with purpose. Nile's story is entertaining, instructive, and inspiring! More importantly, it is convincing in its central message: effective leadership is within reach for all of us. I'm a believer."

—Tom Hill , coauthor *Chicken Soup for the Entrepreneurial Soul, Living at the Summit*, and *Blessed Beyond Measure*

"I have come to believe that character building is much more important than most of what we deliver in the classroom through lectures and textbooks. But developing character in young people is not a straightforward process. I would like to somehow impart to my students the moral courage, patience, trust, and genuine concern for people that—with absolutely no pomposity or pretense—come across in every page of this book. I'll start by suggesting that they read it."

—Edward L. Morris, Professor and former Dean, Lindenwood University; author, *The Lindenwood Model: An Antidote for what Ails Undergraduate Education,* Lindenwood Press, 2007; *Wall Streeters: The Creators and Corruptors of American Finance,* Columbia University Press, 2015

"*Prepare for Leadership* is a fabulous, direct and page-turning view into the life of a man you may not have heard of yet, but whose life lessons you'll never forget. Nile Ramsbottom shares leadership lessons discovered through vast, varied, and amazing experiences from his life. This book will remind you of the power of the human spirit, the gift of faith, the value of character, the impact of service, and the truth that one person can, in fact, be a difference maker. Be prepared to achieve not just your idea of success after reading *Prepare for Leadership*, but more importantly true significance."

—John O'Leary, www.RisingAbove.com

PREPARE *for* LEADERSHIP

From farm boy to Times Square

NILE RAMSBOTTOM
with Russell Stuart Irwin

501 High Street, Ste. A
Boonville, Missouri 65233
660-882-9898
www.MissouriLife.com

Cover art: Russell Stuart Irwin
Book design: Sarah Herrera
All interior images: Courtesy of the Ramsbottom family collection
Managing editor: Danita Allen Wood

ISBN 978-0-9749341-8-1
First Printing: 2015

This book was created and printed in the United States of America.

ACKNOWLEDGMENTS

Everyone I have ever spent time with has had an effect on my life, and therefore, this book. My parents, grandparents, aunts, uncles, cousins, high school friends, and team-mates, all deserve recognition not possible to give in this small space, but I appreciated each one of you.

Some specific people and groups stand out as those I must mention and thank:

Topping the list is my loving wife and best friend, Terry. And my three sons, Greg, Mike, and Matt, have been my "pride and joy" for many years. My life has been further blessed by two daughters-in-law, Darla and Daphne, and by Terry's three sons, Kevin, Craig, and Aaron, and their spouses, Christine, Stacey, and Melissa. Our wonderful grandchildren, Amanda, Katy, Aubrey, Logan, Sydney, Trinity, Abby, Max, and Asher are all treasures. (The world is yours!)

Thanks to my sister, Cathy Garrett, and her husband, Jim, who helped keep child-hood memories accurate.

Though now deceased, my older brother, Jay, was a good influence I am thankful for.

Simpson College provided an opportunity to learn, grow, and put into action some of that knowledge gained. I thank all my friends then and today.

Purina gave me the opportunity to learn, observe, grow, and serve. Over the years of my employment there, many people helped me immensely. I owe them a lot. Some names stand out: Ed Cordes, Jim Hogan, Jim Lepine, Bill Bower, Dub Jones, Bob Reeves, Ed McMillan, Arnie Sumner, Sheila Oliver, and Kelly Patterson.

The West Central Co-op employees and board members offered me an opportunity in a second career. A number of these people also helped start Renewable Energy Group. I asked employees for dedication, trust, passion, and hard work. They provided these attri-butes and more. They were and still are friends. Some names stand out: Jeff Stroburg, My-ron Danzer, Matt Schultes, Jon Scharingson, Natalie Lischer Merrill, Randy Daniels, Gary Haer, Dave Elsenbast, Dan Oh, Brad Albin, Jason Schwenneker, Paul Nees, Dave Slade, Alicia Clancy, Alisha Warnke McAlister, Derek Winkel, Bev Tierney, and Don Nelson.

Many others are and were the driving force each and every day—my sincere thanks to each of you.

The veterans helped by our organization, God Cares, are so worthy and have taught me much about sacrifice. I am thankful for your friendship.

Mark and Todd Simmons, as well as my fellow board members and the employees of Simmons Foods have taught me about the food industry. Thank you, my friends.

Many thanks to my friends, Gary Baker, Tom Hill, and John O'Leary, for the encour-agement that resulted in this book, and without which I would not have pursued getting my story in print.

Special thanks to my partner in writing this book, Russell Irwin, whose gift in writing is second to none. He is also a tremendously talented artist, and the one who created the cover art. I also owe thanks to those that read the early draft of the book and gave me input and encouragement. They are Gordon Moen, Ed Morris, David Sauerburger, Gary Baker, Tom Hill, John O'Leary, Randy Ehret, Mark Whitaker, Lee Kreh, John Welter, Chuck Blossom, Tom Stevener, Bob Cranston, Brad Ford, and Dan Hughes. Thanks to each of you.

Thanks also to Greg Wood and everyone at *Missouri Life* Publishing for believing in and getting behind this story, to *Missouri Life* Art Director Sarah Hererra for designing the book, to Ed Morris for his excellent advisory editing, and to Jeanette Littleton and Danita Allen Wood for editing services.

And last but not least, to the many friends in Missouri, Arizona, and Iowa whom we thoroughly enjoy; we appreciate each of you and your friendship.

A man plans his way, but the Lord guides his steps.
PROVERBS 16:9

To my parents, Clair and Dorothy Ramsbottom, who prepared me with a great example of what loving teamwork and respect look like.

FOREWORD

When Nile Ramsbottom asked me to take a look at his manuscript for the business memoir he was writing, I was hesitant. Books written by retired executives about their careers tend to present a heroic narrative, and I wasn't sure I wanted to commit to reading a few hundred pages of self-aggrandizement. But Nile, the consummate gentleman, has such an unassuming manner that I thought his book might be different. Besides, I knew—only from others—that he was formerly a top executive at Ralston Purina who went on to lead a highly successful enterprise called the Renewable Energy Group. Truth be told, I was a little nosy to find out what REG was all about.

I am so thankful I agreed to his request!

Prepare for Leadership, even in its early draft form, was a most satisfying read. On one level, the book has great inspirational appeal—Nile has done well by doing good. On another level, I enjoyed the clear and interesting way the book explains business transactions. As a former executive vice-president of Stifel, Nicolaus & Co, I found his descriptions of the commodities markets and the initial public offering of REG right-on. Anyone wanting an insider's look at how our financial institutions and markets function will enjoy fascinating, firsthand descriptions in *Prepare for Leadership.*

Yet, I think the greatest value of the book comes from its lessons about leadership and character.

Now in my own second career as a business professor, I think a great deal about how effective business leaders are trained. I have come to believe that character building is much more important than most of what we deliver in the classroom through lectures and textbooks. But developing character in young people is not a straightforward process. I would like to somehow impart to my students the moral courage, patience, trust, and genuine concern for people that—with absolutely no pomposity or pretense—come across in every page of this book. I'll start by suggesting that they read it.

Edward L. Morris

Professor and former Dean, Lindenwood University;
author, *The Lindenwood Model: An Antidote for what Ails Undergraduate Education,*
Lindenwood Press, 2007, and
author, *Wall Streeters: The Creators and Corruptors of American Finance,*
Columbia University Press, 2015

INTRODUCTION

Opportunity and responsibility are what achieved dreams are made of. They are placement and mobility on the road to success. And with them, we expect difficulty. It is implied in their definitions. Even the most optimistic dreamer imagines success by conquest of challenges inherent to opportunity and increasing responsibility. That's the heroic nature of it, the part distinguishing a dream from a nap, or boredom. Anyone can merely proceed from one day to the next. The dreamer dares to do something with each day. Facing difficulty in pursuit of the dream is what's memorable, inspiring, and worthy of celebration when the dream is reached.

But what happens when opportunity is real and near and overwhelmingly huge? What if responsibility feels like questions highlighting inadequacies?

If you have ever found yourself feeling overwhelmed and faced with those kinds of questions, recall this noble reference point: you are the one who dared take the leap. Hopefully you were prepared. If not … well, you will be next time. Even when we fail, pursuit of success offers that education. The key is to keep trying.

I have pursued some dreams—some lofty dreams. Without fail, those travels intersected marvelous opportunities. Also without fail, those opportunities introduced daunting responsibilities. I've been as prone as anyone to the usual reactions: blank staring, forgetting to exhale, looking around to see if someone more capable might be raising their hand to volunteer for the job, and so on. You name it; I've experienced the tendency. But thankfully, more often than not, one reliable tendency overruled the others and kicked in—preparation.

Perhaps you're not so much interested in a great story of courage, persistence, teamwork, and relationships that result in historic accomplishment with global impact. Maybe you only picked up this book for some takeaways on leadership. If that is the case, I can save you some time with this concise summary of the leadership content:

Preparation is the basis of confidence and calm in every circumstance, and confidence is the key to decisiveness.

There you have it, a bit of philosophy that has served me well my entire life. This book is an account of how it has done so. As such, it has no personal value greater than memoirs. And that would not be value enough for me to bother writing a book at all. No, I am after something more. If no one else has taken the trouble to do it, I want to teach you how preparation makes all the difference when it comes to opportunity and responsibility … and therefore, success in leadership. That much I can guarantee you will find in these pages. What I can't guarantee, but hope you will receive as a bonus, is direction concerning your purpose, the very purpose you were destined by God to discover.

Nile D. Ramsbottom

ONE · *Biodiesel*

Boom!

When the explosion occurred, I was in my office, 150 yards away in another building with several insulated walls separating my desk and the blast. Yet it was loud enough for me to hear.

My mouth went dry. I rose from my desk chair, grabbed my hard hat, and dashed to the biodiesel plant.

At the scene of the disaster, I saw the outside contractor who had been welding our tanks lying on the floor, badly injured. No one else sustained any injury—besides emotional trauma. And there was plenty of that!

Within moments, an ambulance was on-site, and medics tended to the injured contractor. He had been blown off a platform and landed on the concrete fifteen feet below. His evident wounds were burns and multiple fractures. We wouldn't know about other injuries until we got him to the emergency room at the local hospital.

As I tried to handle the situation quietly—to at least keep everyone calm enough for the medics to work—a few employees came to me to resign. They weren't just rattled; they were "finished."

"I'm done … I'm outta here! I can't work around this stuff."

"I knew it! I knew this was more dangerous than anyone was letting on. I don't want anything to do with biodiesel. I quit!"

"I'm sorry, Nile, but I've got a wife and kids at home. I didn't sign on for this."

I didn't accept any resignations that day. Instead, I asked all employees to defer all decisions until after we found out exactly what had happened. Over the following days, everyone had their say, everyone was heard, and my ability to hold everyone together was severely tested.

Executing managerial responsibilities in an orderly manner kept my mind off my own internal reactions, helping me hide them from everyone else.

I might want out of this, too. Do I really want anything to do with biodiesel?

***

Biodiesel is made by forced chemical reaction of lipids (animal fats or vegetable oil) using methanol (a flammable, colorless simple alcohol: carbon monoxide, carbon dioxide, and hydrogen) to separate glycerin from the original feedstock substance. A catalyst (such as sodium hydroxide) speeds up the reactive process. Next, the fluid is washed to remove the catalyst and glycerin byproduct; then, the water from the washing phase must be removed. From there, the refinement process focuses on purification. The result is mono-alkyl esters of long-chain fatty acids—biodiesel—useful to run diesel engines, usually as a mixture with petroleum diesel.

When I was introduced to biodiesel, it was made by moving everything from batch to batch to batch (such as 1,000 gallons). Because methanol, a key component of the process, is combustible, highly specific and systematic security measures were necessary throughout the production process.

As dangerous as it all sounds, the benefits of biodiesel warranted efforts to perfect its production, expand its use, and broaden its availability. Biodiesel is a clean-burning, renewable, nature-friendly diesel fuel.

° ° ° °◦▬▬▬◉▬▬▬◦° ° ° °

The plant had been shut down for repair work when the blast occurred. We had strict security procedures in place. We had sign-offs for approval and danger zones that were off limits. Though the contractor had a permit to do specific work in an approved section of the plant, for some reason he had decided to work in an unauthorized area. The tank he'd chosen to work on contained methanol vapors. He was working with a welding torch …

That was a tough day to be in charge. While it was not the company's fault or mine, and any blame was indirect, it all felt direct because of the position of responsibility the company and I were in. And no conciliatory words changed the fact that a man was lying on the floor badly injured.

Thankfully, after a long stay in the hospital, he was OK. The man had survived the explosion.

It remained to be seen if the company would.

Investigations into the circumstances showed that the policies we had in place were good ones. But more layers of accountability were needed to make absolutely sure nothing like that could ever happen again.

A colossal failure can still lead to success.

The timing of the incident was especially difficult. We had worked so hard to get to this point of knowing we were headed in the right direction, the direction of sustained viability. So far, it had been an exercise in overcoming obstacles, especially the reputation of biodiesel production as being a few guys in a shed with vats and batches of "who knows what?" and "who knows how dangerous?"

We had turned the corner and were headed in the direction of a sophisticated, profitable operation. The explosion threatened to eliminate the distance we'd put between ourselves and the back-yard-brew persona and undo the rest of our progress.

To go forward required a new plant, one actually designed and built for biodiesel production. It would be an enormous job with an outrageous price tag. We needed all the credibility we could earn—not explosions. It was either admit defeat and shut things down or learn from error and move on, the better for it and all the more determined.

I was facing one of the greatest tests of my life, professionally and personally, requiring me to apply every leadership quality I'd developed through all of my previous experiences, such as listening, persevering, being transparent, and of course, being prepared.

The route by which I came to be in that biodiesel fuel plant the day of the explosion—or became involved with biodiesel at all—is not what you might expect.

TWO · *Blondie*

The wind in southwest Iowa is sweeping. There's not a lot to obstruct or redirect its path, so it has its way there. It sweeps across open fields as if emptiness exists for it to fill. There is ground, there is the sky above, and there is wind whipping around in between, making noise, and stirring up things.

I think wind likes Iowa. It has a function there, maybe even a mission—sweeping wind hardens the ground. It has partners in its work. Baking beneath the sun in the summer, packed Iowa soil that has not been churned by a farmer's plow is like kiln-fired earthenware. In winter, the deep-freezing bitter cold makes soil like rock. Hard Iowa ground is a good place to learn your manners.

I wondered if she knew how hard the ground was.

"Do you hate me? Why do you keep doing that? I wish I could throw you down on the ground ... see how you like it!"

Only ten years old, I felt a lot of frustration. I shed a lot of tears. But nothing caused her to change. I would look up at her amazed that all my love and affection could continue returning nothing but abuse.

"What have I ever done to you? What have I done but spent all my time with you ... try every way I know to get along?"

Bruised elbows, bruised knees, bruised rumpus, a knot on the noggin now and then, often having the wind knocked out of me, and some really hurt feelings ... who would've thought the beauty I was smitten with could be so ornery? A buckskin quarter horse with black mane and tail, Blondie was my first horse. And she was an education on four legs.

Every time I relaxed, thinking we were finally getting somewhere with the training, she would stop short, lower her head, and toss my bony self like an unwanted cargo projectile. In flight, I was hit by the shock that this had happened again—so as I landed, the one-two punch always left me feeling angry and confused. This combination of negatives was evidently well suited for my temperament because it inspired persistence and forged a resolve to win. And Blondie made sure I understood my winning could only happen with patient investment in trust.

When my father had gotten the two-year-old mare for me, he'd simply turned her over with the words, "Make sure she stays away from my crops, my hogs, and my cattle." He'd left me to figure out how to deal with her on my own.

> Winning requires persistence.

Something about horses appealed to me so much that I would not rest until I had one. I may have thought a horse would understand me better than others. From age four to twelve, I stuttered significantly. This was humiliating, sometimes even traumatic. Maybe this frailness of my humanity

25

inclined me toward finding some outlet for expressing empathy and care.

Wherever it came from, the initial infatuation grew into a deepening love in spite of many pride- and flesh-wounding collisions with the ground.

My older brother, Jay, was not at all into horses. Our dad and he shared an affinity for cars and spent their evenings and weekends tinkering together under one hood or another for hours and hours. To say they were both mechanically inclined would be a gross understatement. Be it tractor, truck, car, motorcycle, generator, or water heater, there was nothing they couldn't fix, overhaul, reconfigure, and improve. I didn't have the same passion or natural ability in that area, so joining their tool-time bonding was not a comfortable fit for any of us, especially me. In its own strange way, this helped steer me toward discovering what fascinated me the way nuts and bolts and pistons fascinated them.

Check every nuance of your communication.

As I worked with Blondie, I quickly learned the experience was not at all like working with an inanimate vehicle. It was all about the relationship. Horses are personal.

I didn't appreciate it at the time, but that one relationship began my understanding of the one thing all relationships are made of: character. In one way or another, whether by intention or default, relationships develop character based on communication—that is, they are characterized by some form of language and how it is communicated.

Blondie taught me to care about whether or not every nuance of my communication was in character with who we were. She demanded it. Anything out of character resulted in another painful landing on the hard ground.

THREE · *English Influence*

Ramsbottom is an English name. Like many Olde English names, its meaning is habitational. It could identify someone as being from the town of Ramsbottom, in Lancashire in the far north of England, or from an agriculturally suitable valley (bottom or Olde English *bopm*). The "ram" part either conveyed a romantic notion (such as valley of the ram) or had nothing at all to do with rams, being derived from the Olde English *hramas* (garlic).

At any rate, the name is of English origin, an ever-present reminder that my family is, too. But, more than just a name, English influence was pervasive in my formative years.

The English are known for their order and etiquette. So our home followed exemplary rules of propriety. Voices were never raised in our home—at least, not by my parents. They were ideal role models for marriage, parenting, and general conduct. They were affectionate and kind toward one another, and I never heard a cross word between them. They enjoyed each other's company.

Discipline, like everything else, followed thoughtful consideration. Never emotional, loud, or angry, it was reasonable and stern—always in that order. I was four years younger than Jay, four years older than our sister, Cathy, and each of us were typical active kids with a penchant for mischief and mishap. But I don't recall either of our parents treating us in any way that could be considered harsh.

Jay's and my rare "punishment" for erring behavior was always a job of some kind, such as cleaning the chicken house. For Cathy, punishment was non-existent, a weakness called "daddy's darling" that may or may not have had English roots! It

> Discipline should follow thoughtful consideration.

was augmented by the fact that Cathy was the only girl in the extended Ramsbottom family—she was the only niece, daughter, granddaughter, anything.

Being used to royal treatment, Cathy was shocked once when, in the course of an argument, I called her a "dirty homo sapien." She was so worked up that she told mom—who only snickered. Cathy felt silly when she discovered the insult merely suggested she might need a bath. And with that, the situation was defused.

Our home was old but kept in tip-top condition. We were not wealthy, but we never had any sense of want or worry, or concern for money or provisions. Our weekly allowances were regular and always sufficient for saving and applying to horse care or car maintenance. I excelled in money management from a young age, and my tin money box was kept in the family desk like a petty cash bank, usually with an IOU or two sticking out of it.

We shared everything from candy bars and eight-ounce A&W Root Beers to the telephone and the TV. Our phone was on a twelve-family party line. I would call my girlfriend when Mom and Dad were gone and lock Cathy out of the family room during the conversation. She would always protest, "Any of our relatives could be listening in ... why not me?"

Since we were the first of our kin to have a television, other people were often in our house gathered around to watch it. Even the neighbors—people my parents knew but I didn't—took the liberty to drop by for some TV viewing. It sometimes felt like we were the ones introducing television to Iowa. Our doors were never locked, so we would come home to a house full of people gathered around our nine-inch TV. It came with a magnifying glass to mount in front of it, so we could view it from a little distance.

In the environs of my youth, that was about it for technological amusement. All other entertainment was self-made and generally outdoors.

In keeping with the historical roots of our name, we were agrarian folks, farmers, landowners. In the early going, our family was on an 80-acre piece of land connected to 320 acres populated by the rest of the Ramsbottoms. Dad bought more and more land over the years, eventually accumulating around 240 acres.

We raised cattle, hogs, and chickens and rotated crops of corn, soybeans, hay, and oats. Jay and I had lots of physically challenging chores that made exhaustion a normal part of life. Cathy had to practice the piano and participated in farming when she wanted to work on her tan. We all grew up driving jeeps, tractors, and other farm vehicles from early adolescence. Sundays were the only downshift from the daily responsibilities of farm life.

We were from the reformation side of the Judeo-Christian traditions of our English heritage, and Mom took us kids to Sunday school every week. Dad stayed home. He never said anything negative about religion, but just didn't participate. Maybe he felt someone needed to be on top of the farm responsibilities with everyone else taking Sunday off—and the someone was him. Whatever the reason, attending our Christmas musicals and a Wednesday night supper now and then was the extent of his church-going. Nevertheless, Christian faith took hold of me in my early life to grow in importance from then on.

The English influence was most noticeable to this middle child in the tradition of firstborn privilege. Jay received the lion's share of our father's time and mentoring, and I often noticed disparity between how my big brother Jay and I were treated.

When he came of age to drive a car, he received a late model vehicle in good condition. When I turned sixteen, I had to purchase my own transportation using allowance money I'd saved. I was able to get a ten-year-old Oldsmobile with rust holes in the fender wells that let in dust on gravel and dirt roads. The interior would become a dust cloud—not exactly a good impression on dates—so I covered the holes by bolting old license plates to the interior of the fenders.

Similarly, when I graduated from high school, there were no family funds to put toward my college aspirations because they had been used up on various educational endeavors Jay had pursued. I was on my own to make college happen.

One of the most painful results of the birth order phenomenon happened during my first year of showing at the Adair County Fair. I was eleven and had proudly owned Blondie for almost a year. I also was old enough to know what a big deal the fair was. County fairs in Iowa are a big annual event rife with long-standing family traditions. Hundreds of people come from miles around to celebrate rural glory.

I had worked hard and was entered with Blondie in two classes of competition: 4-H and Open. I couldn't wait to show off my horse at the fair and to demonstrate how much we had bonded and the progress I'd made under Blondie's training. The opportunity to participate in such a grand event was the most anticipated moment of my young life.

Jay had shown hogs in the fair for several years and knew the basics of how fairs worked. Since this was my first year, it seemed reasonable to assume that Dad would help me. It didn't work out that way. While he was busy working with Jay, I was left to navigate the dense crowds and complicated showing schedule alone. I was there early but couldn't figure out where or when I was to show Blondie. I was too intimidated by the whole situation to know whom to ask. By the time I got the help I needed, it was too late. Blondie and I had missed our scheduled showing in 4-H and Open class. I was devastated.

"All those bumps and bruises and hours of training for nothing," I muttered tearfully to Blondie as we threaded through the crowd and back to the stall, where I stood with my head against her and wept. On that day I was pretty sure she was the only friend I had in the whole world. My debut at the Adair County Fair would have to wait a year.

In times like those, being a part of the larger Ramsbottom family spread throughout a four-hundred-acre piece of Iowa was helpful. In that context I saw that the special blessing upon first-born males was consistent throughout the entire family— grandparents, uncles, cousins. Gifts were universally different for the eldest male in each family, as were other forms of generosity and devotion.

As a result I knew not to take the whole thing personally, which protected me from concluding something self-destructive like, "I am loved less," or "There's something wrong with me … I am of lesser value."

While Jay benefited from the traditional first-born preferential treatment, that did not keep us from enjoying a good relationship. We were, after all, Ramsbottoms: well-bred, generally polite, respectful toward one another, and most important, family.

Nor would it be accurate to say the custom of hierarchical favoritism put me at a disadvantage. They say necessity is the mother of invention. Well, so is compensation. Any shortcomings I faced from not being born first meant I learned to develop resourcefulness and ingenuity. And I learned to keep my eyes open for those who had knowledge and skills I lacked and were inclined to share.

In 1960, at sixteen years old, I had an itch to take my 1950 Oldsmobile to the drag strip in Des Moines and see what the car could do. The National Hot Rod Association managed the track, which had an observation tower, timers, grandstand, and an official flag-waving race starter. This was an auspicious racing debut for a nobody teenager with a ten-year-old car. But my entry was a midsize light body vehicle with

Oldsmobile's famous "Rocket V8," a combination I knew would at least provide an entertaining adrenaline rush or two while speeding down the track.

Jay was home from college that weekend and agreed to help out, along with a couple of his college buddies. We decided we would have the best shot if Jay drove. I felt pretty cool in the company of three twenty-year-olds who knew a thing or two about cars and thought mine was worth spending a day at the track.

But the experience was humiliating at first. It was a hot humid day—especially on the asphalt track. The conditions created a problem with water getting into my Oldsmobile's fuel line. The car performed horribly, sputtering out when Jay hit the gas in each practice run. Since the event looked like it would be a dud, Jay and his two friends left.

My mom sometimes used my car, and I spotted a couple of clothespins she had left in it. I recalled having heard that a wooden clothespin placed on the fuel line near the carburetor would help with vapor lock. It seemed like an old wives' tale to me, but I had nothing to lose. I put both clothespins on the gas line before the carburetor.

Several winning heats later, I was in the final race in my class against a 1955 Ford. After winning that race, I took home a huge trophy to the shock of my brother and his friends.

One of the most remarkable demonstrations of the stoic Ramsbottom strain of English took place during my high school years. My grandfather was a fine man, a good man, and a generous man who was widely respected in our area of Iowa. But he was, well, not very grandfatherly. Our relationship was strictly business. I saw him quite a bit during my growing up years. Besides regular family gatherings, my dad, my brother, and I spent a lot of time helping with the work on Grandpa's property. At those times, Jay and I were clearly there to get things done, not to be enjoyed as grandkids.

I lettered in football all four years of high school. While not exceptional, I was good enough to have a starting spot on the team. That meant something to my grandfather, who it turns out loved and respected me more than I realized. He never missed a single home game of my entire high school football career. He brought his own folding chair to each game and sat by himself, watched the game, and left.

I never knew he was there. He never said a word to me about the games. I would not have expected him to be there because he did not express any interest in football. He only attended the games to watch his grandson, which I didn't learn until my grandma told me many years later.

Tell people when you appreciate them.

The math of human experience is not as simple as two plus two equals four, or two minus two equals zero. I had a great childhood. Yes, at times I felt a dispositional edge of resentment about what seemed like tradition-sanctioned unfairness. But I wore it quietly in keeping with trained English decorum. And, however quiet, *edge* is motivation. Birth order taught me something about myself: I was not a fan of being second.

Lack of a privilege can inspire ingenuity and resourcefulness.

FOUR · *Early Preparation*

Blondie was fast ... very fast. And fast is thrilling. But I didn't have much opportunity to race her and find out just how fast she was. By eleven, I was "one of the men," which meant old enough to drive a tractor and be in the fields helping make the family farm successful. I don't recall a single moment of temptation to debate the issue.

Cathy had an old mare selected for gentleness and predictability, not spirited disposition and speed. But it represented the only racing fun we had from week to week. So I raced Cathy just about every Sunday and on rainy Saturdays when we could break from work in the fields.

"Fast" has a certain look that experienced horse trainers recognize. We were showing in a county fair, and a man asked if I would accept a challenge to race.

Wow, real racing! But I immediately realized I had no idea how fast Blondie could run. Blondie had never been challenged. So I didn't know what her peak speed was or how she would react to racing an unfamiliar competitor. The other unknown factor was how her inexperienced rider would handle the situation.

"Sure," I said, without asking any of the questions someone more experienced would have asked, like, "How far?" or "What's the course?"

My challenger was up to something I had no clue about. The race was being arranged for betting. I was approached because another horse was needed. Other than that, the whole thing was pretty straightforward—a quarter-mile race on a half-mile oval dirt track. My challenger handled the race preparations and set the race up for two o'clock. When two o'clock came around, I learned there were four horses in the race.

Even though it was a spontaneous and unofficial event, the race attracted quite a bit of attention. But I didn't react to that. To some, I might have appeared to be poised beyond my years. Actually, it was just part of the training I'd received from Blondie: nothing out of character.

I was so completely focused on the communication between my horse and me that nerves had no opportunity to mess with me. And because Blondie was attentive to my actions, focused communication also insulated her from distraction.

Keep your focus.

We won the race and found out just how fast Blondie was.

We also discovered how fragile focus is ... or, how important maintaining focus is. The win was exhilarating, which was more distracting than the pre-race activities.

Forgetting about body language communication, I must have done something that sent the wrong message to Blondie. No sooner had we crossed the finish line when she stopped sharp, dropped her head, and dumped me in the dirt right there in front of everyone, competitors zipping by frighteningly close to my tumbling anatomy. Even winning a race with Blondie turned out to be painful and humbling.

Then, I got a lecture from my dad when he learned of the matter. I'd had no idea I was "cavorting with schemers."

But I was not in the least dissuaded from my love of horses, or riding and training them. In horsemanship I had found something I could excel in, something well suited for my relational personality. Whether in the show ring, riding rodeo, or exploring the acreage around our home, I accumulated innumerable stories and meaningful experiences on the backs of horses. And the educational aspect of equestrian husbandry captivated me. Early on, I learned mainly from books. Later, through trial and error and being around experienced horse folks, I discovered that much of what the books taught was wrong. Through it all one thing remained constant: I never tired of thorough caring for each horse and every leather, steel, and textile element of the tack I accumulated, however heavy or small.

Growing up around the horse arena, I saw lots of different styles of handling horses—including various approaches to bullying. They were all effective in some measure, but they were not the best way. They were short-cut approaches to a handler's control, getting his or her way. This often resulted in a horse with a broken spirit, which is not the goal of training a horse. Bullying approaches erred in three primary ways: one was disregarding personality, two was disrespecting the relationship, and three was ignoring nature.

A horse's sight encompasses 320 degrees, pretty close to wrap-around vision so the horse can keep a watch on what is in front, to the sides, and partly to the rear. A horse's awareness of its surroundings is its first order of nature and first capacity of defense, triggering flight. So horses are naturally skittish about any kind of erratic behavior. Relating to a horse personally—as with any relationship—calls for respect of facts of nature. Patience, consistent actions (no erratic behavior), and awareness of creature comforts that affect behavior (food, water, hooves free of debris) all return the rewards of familiarity and trust.

Trust is the most important factor in a relationship with a horse. It is the goal informing every action. When my dad brought Blondie home, I fed her, brushed her, and cared for her for weeks and weeks before ever riding her. Heart investment came first. It was the basis for the development of trust.

It takes a lot to establish trust. It doesn't take much to hurt it. And damage to trust is damage to relational character.

When I was seventeen, I was participating in a weekend horse show. My riding resume showed some success, and I felt pretty full of myself. Extra activities outside the ring led to unexpected difficulty with my horse in the ring. I got aggressive and tried to force my will upon her:

It doesn't take much to damage trust.

"You get straightened up here! I'm the boss. I trained you better than that!"

It confused the horse, which responded as if to say, "Who is this guy? How did I get a different handler today?"

Those few minutes in the ring contradicted everything previously conveyed between me and the horse and cost weeks of relational repair, including lots of backtracking and recovery.

Aggression and bullying won't convey the intended message.

I learned over the years that the message received through aggression, bullying, and erratic actions is never what you think it will be. Its product is never the "discipline" intended. In fact it is the opposite of discipline: nothing knowable or predictable, just whatever emotional response occurs in the moment. Trust is lost and replaced with confusion and fear. It's a high price to pay after all the investment of relational bonding.

As I continued working on my horse-handling skills, I paid more attention to cultivating a relationship. Before long, I was feeling like a horse expert. Those days proved inspirational, insuring that horses would be a big part of my life from then on. I had Blondie bred and eventually raised, broke, trained, showed, and traded five of her offspring. With some help from my dad, breaking, training, trading, and selling horses became my primary source of income and a nice bit of savings built throughout my high school years. It would ultimately pay for part of my college tuition.

Dad was initially that adult presence discouraging any scheme aimed at taking advantage of my youth. He also taught me a thing or two about the art of negotiation, about knowing and abiding by real value.

By the time I was sixteen, negotiating was becoming second nature to me. Once, after agreeing to let a friend borrow my motorcycle, I wrote a contract for him to sign. It had a schedule of reimbursement payments should anything happen to my property and stated my willingness to accept payment in a horse

Learn the art of negotiating.

of equal value to the motorcycle. Simple as it was, it signified things to come. In the years that followed, I would fashion and enter many contractual agreements.

Negotiations, contracts, relationships, trust ... all of these were indicators. They were essentials of a career still several years in the future.

The career focus—management—also had an early inspiration. One of my jobs on the farm was shoveling manure in the hog houses. Habit dictated that I was in a hog house doing that job around three in the afternoon when my Dad headed to town in his Jeep every day. I would look out from the hog house between shovels of manure and watch him drive off, knowing his destination was the local coffee shop. As I saw it, that was Dad's religion, time to hang out with friends, "fellowship," chat over a cup of coffee.

One day I jokingly asked, "Dad, what is happening in town every day right at the time the manure needs shoveling here on the farm?"

"Well, you see, Nile," he answered thoughtfully, "we're running a pretty significant farming operation here. Some serious responsibilities are associated with that ... banking, administration, accounting, business. I have to go into town to take care of those things."

"Oh, OK, so what do you call that part of the business?" I replied.

"Son, that's management."

With the smell of fresh manure still clinging to my nostrils, I responded, "That's what I'm going to be some day, a manager."

FIVE · *Marriage*

I was in love with a young lady when I was seventeen, and I was fairly certain she was "the one." Her mother didn't want her dating any more ... or at least, not dating me. So she forced an end to our relationship. Not long afterward, the girl attempted suicide. Thankfully she lived. But she faced a long battle with emotional distress and illness. In those days, there were no cell phones, messaging, or emails. All our communication with each other was terminated. When she was finally well again, her father's employer transferred him to another location. I never saw her again.

I handled the experience poorly, constantly looking back and wondering what I could have done differently. I was cut off from the girl I loved and had no response. I just shut down and let it all happen. Should I have done something valiant, fought for her and for our relationship? I had no way to see the situation coming, so I couldn't prepare. Just fell in love ... I don't know when I have felt so powerless, before or since.

Shortly afterward, another young lady, Marge, pursued me. Still stunned by the earlier situation, I reacted poorly again, passive, though in a different way. A year and a half into the relationship, we eloped—during the summer between my freshman and sophomore years of college. We weren't trying to make any rebellious, counter-culture statement. We just did it. Boom—married!

It hurt my parents deeply that I would get married in a way that disregarded them. No planning, no wise counsel, no family involvement, no excitement, no celebration, no propriety. It was a very unRamsbottom way to go about things, and they took it personally. I was once again cut off—not from the girl this time, but from my own parents. Just like that—almost no communication!

I resumed some contact with my mom after months of disconnection, but it was nothing like the warm relationship of the past. And where my dad was concerned, the alienation was stark and unyielding.

These were trying times when I could have used some parental encouragement and direction. Full-time work and full-time education left little time for Marge and me to just be young and married. I gave up a football scholarship at Simpson College because I needed a full-time job to support the two of us while I also focused on school. The job I landed was a good one, running the offset printing department for a printing company near the college. Because they liked my work and eventually trusted me with the keys to the building, the owners of the company let me set my own hours to accommodate my studies.

When someone makes a mistake is when they most need encouragement and guidance.

Nevertheless, the job was not quite enough to cover all of our expenses. We faced tremendous financial strain. I once left for school in the morning knowing we were down to our last five dollars. When I arrived at home later, there was a barbeque grill on the back porch that my wife had bought at a garage sale with our last five dollars. I couldn't help but stammer at her enthusiasm over a new grill for which we had no use because we had no money for food to cook on it. It was a time when several major decisions of my early manhood looked questionable.

Most of the friends I grew up with followed family tradition and pursued agricultural degrees in college. But I had seen enough of agriculture and wanted to learn about something else. I had hopes of being a businessman, so I studied economics and business administration.

The college years passed quickly, but a pleasant surprise awaited me at the end of my senior year. After I finished one of my finals in the last semester, the professor invited me to walk with him as he headed to the "great hall." When we got there, I discovered a ceremony was being held in my honor. I was presented with *The Wall Street Journal* Award for the highest cumulative four-year grade-point average in the Business School. I had no idea I was in the running for anything, so it was quite a shock.

I had started my college career as a farm boy who didn't know if he had the tools to make it. I not only made it at the collegiate level but was moving on with this solid vote of confidence about my ability to succeed out there where my real dreams were: in the world of business. I never suspected that would lead me right back to agriculture. I would soon be immersed in the ag industry.

And something besides graduating from college would bring big changes—much bigger than finding my way into a career in business. I didn't learn of it until the latter part of my senior year. Marge was pregnant with our first child. Life was getting really exciting!

Not everything was bright and hopeful, however. Through those college years, I hadn't accomplished a reconciliation between my parents and me. Mom and I were communicating some, but still much less than before the eloping offense. And silence prevailed between my dad and me—that would remain for a long time.

SIX · *Essential Ingredients*

The wind in St. Louis is heavy, weighted with humidity. This has something to do with the way the city is situated on the Mississippi, between it and the Meramec and Missouri rivers. And like every other element of the weather patterns between there and the Ozark foothills to the west, the wind is known for its unpredictable extremes in variation. One minute, it's kicking like an ol' Missouri Mule; the next it's as still and stubborn as one, withholding the slightest movement when a breeze would give welcome relief from a damp, suffocating summer atmosphere.

Along the banks of the Mississippi in St. Louis, Missouri, William Danforth started making mule feed in 1894. The company he founded, Purina Wholefood Company, did well, quickly expanding its production to a wide range of domestic animal feed.

But Danforth was not satisfied with his success keeping livestock well nourished. He wanted to further expand into the human food market with a cereal brand.

To get past his fame as the animal feed guy, he needed an endorsement to bolster marketing. He sought and found it in an eccentric social revolutionary by the name of Webster Edgerly.

Originally an attorney, Edgerly was the founder of Ralstonism, a utopian movement promising telepathic powers and longevity through principles of "magnetism" and good health management. More importantly, Ralstonism had a following of eight hundred thousand people. And as part of Edgerly's writings on dietary practice, he promoted consumption of cereal much like Danforth's creation.

With Edgerly's endorsement, William Danforth's new cereal was a tremendous success. In 1902 he changed the name of his company to Ralston-Purina. On the Ralston side, focus on human and pet food products would lead to a place among the most successful companies in those industries. The Purina side would remain devoted to its roots in animal and poultry feed products and become the largest producer of animal and poultry feed in the world.

Mule chow and quirky cultic utopianism were not the typical paths to establishment for the most prominent Fortune 500 companies of the twentieth century. But Ralston-Purina's growth sustained lofty status long after Ralstonism lost its momentum and history had all but erased Edgerly's connection to the company.

On June 15, 1966, I joined Ralston Purina. It seemed like I'd stepped right off the stage after receiving my college diploma and into a career. But the two phases of my life were actually separated by one month.

I hired into a management-training program and was told to expect a geographical move every few years. The first assignment was close to home: Iowa Falls, Iowa. Though it was comfortable and familiar geographically, we knew no one in and nothing about Iowa Falls. The timing of the relocation was not the best. Marge was far along in her pregnancy. We were moving to a place where she had no established prenatal care. Our first priority was to find an obstetrician. We tried the one doctor recommended by her previous doctor, but he didn't have room for a new patient. One by one, other doctors we contacted also declined taking on a new patient mid-pregnancy.

That part of the move made it stressful. In fact, I was panicked. *What did I do to my young family?*

In what felt like a last chance, we called on a Catholic clinic of three young doctors. One of them, Dr. Donley, accepted Marge as his patient. They immediately developed a trusting rapport that relieved all the stress. It could not have been a better outcome to our dilemma.

On September 9, 1966, having a child went from an exciting anticipation to a wonderful addition to our home and the world named Greg. I needed no preparation for proud papa. That came naturally. And I was introduced to a new kind of responsibility, one that changed and blessed me in ways I could never have expected: fatherhood.

<hr />

While "management" as the program focus of Ralston Purina's management training program meant what I expected in some ways—management of facilities, operations, people, and so on—I was soon to learn it included an unexpected area of discipline: management of risk.

Purina was one of the most prominent commodities traders in the world, purchasing five million tons of feedstock a year. Without managing or protecting financial positions, the five-million-ton investment could be a short track to ruin if the market in a given year were to take an unexpected turn in an undesired direction.

Of course, having grown up on a farm, I knew that commodities were hard assets like the ones we grew and raised—corn, soybeans, hogs, cattle—but I never thought much about the two non-agricultural categories of commodities: fuels and metals.

A degree in economics and business administration supplied that bit of information, along with the fundamentals of supply and demand. College further provided some knowledge of basic concepts of a global economy. Yet I had no reason to fully understand the specifics there. I didn't know it at the time, but the new job was the beginning of the real education.

I joined Ralston Purina during an era of seemingly random diversification. Continental Baking Company (Wonder Bread and Hostess products), Chex cereal, Keystone Ski Resorts in Colorado, Van Camp seafood products, a sports and entertainment arena in St. Louis called the Checkerdome, and the St. Louis Blues hockey team were among properties under the umbrella of the checkerboard logo. The logo itself was of great importance, having become one of the five most valuable brands in the country. My career identity would be tied to that logo for

Management of risk is part of management.

the next thirty-three years.

Though my career began in Iowa geographically, it was guided by executive decisions made at the corporate headquarters in St. Louis. The sense of observation and direction from above, hierarchically speaking, made a profound impression. Someone was watching my career, making decisions to ensure a comprehensive education and upward trajectory. This became more evident as my career with Ralston Purina moved along. While geographical assignments would span from the Deep South to the Upper Northwest and cover several Midwestern stops in between, a cultivated identity was rooted in St. Louis, Ralston Purina's corporate home.

Ralston Purina was known for its strong development culture. In fact, its structured training program was admired, envied, and watched closely by other prominent companies—management of other companies in related industries kept an eye on trainees, hiring them away from Ralston around the two-year mark of the company's investment.

As my first training station, Iowa Falls was a strategic location. The initial phase of management training was an eighteen-month program thoroughly exposing trainees to the two primary functions of the business: feed manufacturing and soybean processing.

Iowa Falls was home to an animal and poultry feed manufacturing and soybean processing plant. The facilities sprawled across twenty acres of land, providing an experience that included rotating through every phase of the dual manufacturing complex. I was also introduced to every facet of management—purchasing, accounting, manufacturing, sales, transportation, and credit.

Rotations through the plant lasted a month, and at the end of each, the trainee wrote a report about what he observed and learned. The report was submitted to the immediate training manager and passed on to the division manager overseeing the trainee's progress from the corporate offices. The same was done on a lengthier and more in-depth level when time in each managerial department was completed.

On one occasion, I was informed that ten people from the corporate headquarters were visiting the plant in a few days. Led by one of the company's top officers, Ed Cordes, they were coming for annual meetings to evaluate how the plant was doing.

Ed Cordes had a reputation as one of those guys a lot of people steered clear of. He did not place a premium on smiling. His toughness was accentuated by a stern look and a gruff manner.

As a trainee who had been there only a handful of months, I assumed my role would be that of observer, and I looked forward to the experience. But on the day before the team's arrival, I learned I would be presenting. The shocking news sent me scrambling to prepare.

A strong development culture is key to a career.

The eve of the meetings, I was told, was poker night—an opportunity to mingle that I should not miss. But I felt the "opportunity" invaded my preparation time. I was not good at poker or eager to play it even under normal circumstances.

Members of the managerial delegation were hard-driving, no-nonsense business people during the day. But I soon learned they also enjoyed a well-earned occasion to play hard. They were people of the world, mostly from large cities. They knew their hard liquor and preferred mixed drinks with a bite, with no dilution of ice. I, on the other hand, could recall having one beer during my entire four-year college career.

Somehow my place at the poker table wound up being next to Ed Cordes, who repeatedly called me Niles throughout the evening—something I didn't appreciate. It was an uncomfortable situation that became more serious as the night wore on. Two things occupied my thoughts: *It's getting late and I have to make a presentation at 7 AM*, and, *Should I correct Ed Cordes on calling me Niles?*

Finally I said, "Mr. Cordes, it's Nile, without the s."

The room quieted for a moment before the poker resumed.

Sometime after midnight, Ed announced it was time for a winner-take-all round to close the night. As the cards were dealt, Ed received two kings, usually hard to beat in those circumstances. But my fourth and fifth cards were aces. I wound up winning the pot, and Ed Cordes turned to me and said, "I don't care what your name is … you'll always be Niles to me!"

The presentation went well the next day. The high point was when I survived tense moments answering some of Ed's signature fire-breathed questions. He later mentioned the nerve of a trainee correcting him on name pronunciation in front of his staff.

Have the courage to speak up.

From that time we shared a good rapport. But it was more a result of how much I came to respect Ed Cordes than anything that went on during an evening of poker. I particularly respected his toughness. So unlike others, I had no reason to avoid him.

○ ○ ○ ○━━━━◉━━━━━○ ○ ○ ○

I must have been getting along pretty well in the training cycle because right after my one-year anniversary, I was ordered to prepare to move on. My eighteen-month training in Iowa Falls was cut short so I could fill a purchasing position in Louisville, Kentucky. Within a month, that's where I and my young family were living.

Not only had we left Iowa, but we had crossed the Mississippi! And for Marge, something about moving beyond the Mississippi meant really far away, making that move especially difficult for her and a stressful time for us.

○ ○ ○ ○━━━━◉━━━━━○ ○ ○ ○

Louisville was a soybean processing plant with three distinct industry focuses: feed, edible, and industrial. I had already been introduced to the larger feed part of the business at the training plant in Iowa. This was more specialized: soybean meal processing for use in feed products.

Edible and industrial were completely new to me. "Edible" meant edible protein for humans—specifically, soy-based high protein food for babies, like that used in baby formula. "Industrial" meant soybean meal processed for industrial purposes. The industry served by the Louisville plant was the paper industry. The product was the soy-based coating that gives paper a smoother surface with better absorption of ink for writing and printing.

The official title of my position at the Iowa Falls plant was assistant buyer. In Louisville, I was promoted to buyer. Not only was it another entirely different level of exposure to Ralston's vast industrial complex, it was my first taste of direct responsibility. I was no longer a trainee being educated. I was now in a position and expected to produce accomplishment. That is how the Ralston Purina development culture worked. Movement was highly calculated and detail specific. Every move meant a promotion. And every promotional step was an introduction to new territorial functions and greater responsibility.

As a buyer working in the soybean processing division, I began to discover my forte within Purina: merchandising. But someone higher up, someone at the company headquarters in St. Louis had already recognized it. I had several mentors along the way. But the most consistent were Jim Hogan and Ed Cordes, two of the top six officers in the company. I suspected Ed Cordes was making the majority of decisions. Whoever it was, the decisions were directing me along a career path designed for my abilities to flourish to the mutual benefit of the company and me.

In Louisville, I got my real introduction to purchasing commodities, which inherently included risk management—hedging. To put it another way: part of my job in Louisville was an education in sophisticated market practices. I was twenty-three years old, and it was heady stuff. I knew it was a rare continuing education not easily come by, and an opportunity many bright and talented professionals would envy. More than duty, making the most of my opportunity became a matter of identity.

As I started out at as a buyer in Louisville, my knowledge of trading commodities was like that of a person recalling some words and their definitions after taking only a year of Spanish to satisfy a foreign language requirement.

I knew, for example, that derivatives were financial contracts that derive their value from underlying real assets. But I did not know about futures contracts. And I had a pedestrian appreciation of hedging as an offsetting investment (like buying gold because gold keeps its value when the dollar loses its value). These were crude insights at best. Suddenly thrust into a position as soybean buyer for a major industry player, I had a lot to learn.

Over a century had passed since centralized trading of commodities contracts had been introduced at the Chicago Board of Trade. But I might as well have been born a century before those facts and their significance. I was clueless. The new job would transform my ignorance into an intimate understanding of the commodities marketplace. But first, I had to become an expert in the soybean market.

Soybeans were the second largest volume ingredient across the spectrum of Ralston Purina's animal feed products. As I learned to thoroughly understand the soybean division, that led to knowing about the entire animal feed division, which was a later step in Purina's hierarchical structure.

I was a true student of my discipline, absorbing every nuance of information relevant to our internal operations and our market. Nevertheless, the education was intense. I often felt I was not learning as much information as I should, especially concerning risk management.

The animal feed industry (domestic farm animals excluding dogs and cats) is fiercely competitive. Purina Mills had 10 percent of the industry. Every animal type has basic nutritional needs at each stage of life. Our customers were farmers trying to make a living off the animals, so the animal's food intake was the customer's primary concern.

The farmer is on narrow margins selling to variable seasonal markets. A farmer with 100 head of cattle on feed for 120 days wants to secure a quote for a feed product that is set for the duration of that time period because feed cost is the basis of the customer's profit calculations. On the supply side of that equation, Purina feed stock managers had to buy right in order to provide the customer with a sound quote for profitability within a narrow margin market.

Those quotes for the farmers were based on due diligence in commodity pricing. While the list of ingredients in our feed products was long—more than one hundred ingredients—the primary ones were commodities: corn, soybean meal, wheat and wheat byproducts, oats, cotton seed meal, sunflower meal, peanut meal, animal fat, minerals such as calcium and phosphorous, vitamins, and others. Scientists applied precise nutritional analysis to each ingredient. Biochemists, nutritionists, formulators, and buyers were very quality-conscious and constantly communicating with one another.

"Here is what the animal needs," a scientist would explain, "and here is what's in corn."

Supplying a list of protein sources (soybean meal, peanut meal, etc.) and percentage ranges of proteins from the various sources, a nutritionist would map combinations suitable to the animal's ideal balanced diet. Buyers then worked from lists with ingredient percentage specifications for every feed product.

The buyer's responsibility was to get the highest quality ingredients at the best prices. Source of supply, quality of supply, and delivery of supply were critical to accurately forecast prices—and ensure the company's success.

There were so many details to care for that it would have been easy to think missing one little thing wouldn't be that big of a deal. And this is probably the most common error of mentality in people holding entry-level positions across all industries. I learned early that every conversation deserved my complete attention, every decision must be based on my full intellectual commitment, and every action deserved my very best effort. Yes, those things were matters of function, but even more so of character.

Decisions should be based on full intellectual commitment.

Ingredients! The details matter. Customer care, scientific feed recipes, commodities, purchasing, risk management, material processing, and the component details of each were ingredient parts of a language of applied knowledge. At Ralston

Purina, I was immersed in a training program designed to produce fluency in that language. The language included other essential ingredients, like the trust, commitment, integrity, and
productivity ethic first cultivated in the home of my youth.

Become a student of
your discipline.

Command of the language was the basis of company success.
I learned it was also the basis of confidence and calm in every
circumstance. It secured respect among peers, the trust of superiors, and the confidence of customers.

I did not know it then, but the essential ingredients of professional credibility were being developed right there in those introductory location assignments at
Ralston Purina. Equipped with these, I would one day have the opportunity to contribute significantly to the creation of an entire industry.

SEVEN · *A Covert Assignment*

"We have a need in Macon, Georgia."

In 1969, I was just getting to the point of proficiency as Louisville's soybean buyer and loved what I was doing. I may not have exactly taken to commodities trading like a cat to a barn, but I was excited to get to work every day. And I was catching on. It was enough progress in Louisville. My superiors had other plans for me.

Marge and I liked Louisville and the surrounding area, so we were not thrilled to learn that I was needed in the Deep South … and would be moving there almost immediately. And the news was delivered with an odd attachment.

"The most important thing down in Macon is what's going on in transportation. The guy handling logistics down there does not communicate well with us. We're not saying anything shifty is going on. We just don't really know what the situation is. As you will see, transportation is a big deal in Macon. We need some insight."

Settling in to a comfort zone was antithetic to the Ralston Purina development culture. That was explained clearly when I signed on in the manager trainee program. So I was prepared to adjust. Initially, the assignment appeared to be a lateral career move. But I soon realized it could be a real boon to my upward mobility. I was selected to handle something concerning the people at corporate. My supervisor's approach to explaining the dual assignment was matter-of-fact.

"Macon is a feed manufacturing facility. For the most part, it's stuff you've already seen. And your position will be the same: buyer. That will remain your primary responsibility. We know you enjoy working in commodities. You can keep your hand in that. But as an added duty, we want you to investigate transportation."

I had shown some affinity for handling the complexities of the transportation side of purchasing in Louisville and assumed that was why I got the Macon assignment. But the word "investigating" connected to my job description was a little unsettling. To have a dual focus at my new post was no big deal. But stealthily looking at how one of the department heads there handled things seemed like a role that could be stressful.

While I would work directly for the Macon plant manager, I would also secretly work for the corporate folks in St. Louis. My immediate supervisor told me the dual role was unprecedented. Since the plant manager would be unaware of my primary reason for being sent there, I felt as if I were involved in an episode of *Mission Impossible.*

That wasn't the only unsettling part of the introduction to my transfer to Macon.

"Being an Iowa native, you probably don't know a lot about the Deep South," my supervisor cautioned me. "There are a few things you need to be prepared for. Segregation is still a big deal down there. Don't be surprised to see separate drinking fountains and restrooms for whites and blacks. If you are walking down the sidewalk and a black person is walking in front of you, he or she will likely step onto the street to give you rights to the sidewalk for passing. If you're in a checkout line at a store and blacks are ahead of you, be prepared for the clerk to wave you ahead of them to be checked out first. No need to take issue with it. That's just the way it is down there."

Hearing those words of warning from my superiors I realized my naiveté. They were right about my exposure to racism growing up in Iowa. In the eighteen years leading up to college, I recall crossing paths with exactly one black student. During the college years, I met two or three more, and in the few years since then, it had been the same.

No one I knew ever spoke of blacks or black-white issues. I had not been exposed to interracial dynamics enough to develop an opinion of any kind, let alone a prejudicial disposition. What I knew of matters related to segregation came from the national news I had read and seen on TV. They had always seemed far away ... more relevant to the experience of other people in other places.

Yet, the Civil Rights Movement, aimed at eradicating segregation, was like a backdrop to the years of my young adulthood. In the early 1960s, highly publicized protests in Birmingham, Alabama, Jackson, Mississippi, and other cities throughout the South made it clear that the movement was gaining momentum toward some definitive resolve. The assassination of Martin Luther King on April 4, 1968, and the rioting that followed during the "Holy Week Uprising" seemed even then a pivotal moment in our nation's history. Only a few months later, on June 6, Robert Kennedy, an ardent supporter of the Civil Rights Movement, was also assassinated.

I was thankful for the heads-up from supervisors about the conditions I would encounter in the South, but it contributed to an unsettled feeling about where I was headed.

The transportation supervisor in Macon was tall and rough looking, reminding me of the former President of France, Charles de Gaulle. At least part of the communication issue that corporate struggled with was the fact that he simply did not communicate. He didn't strike me as shy, just extremely non-verbal. Had they been written out, his responses to my communication attempts wouldn't have warranted punctuation because they were one or two syllable answers at best. I would get nowhere with my investigation by asking him questions.

Thankfully, there were other ways to look into the transportation situation that fit nicely with my purchasing position. Transportation expenses fell within the scope of the buyer's responsibilities. Doing business in large numbers of material tonnage was a big part of the expense. So I was relieved to discover I could handle both of my Macon assignments without conflict.

The transportation pricing system was complicated in Macon. In other locations throughout the country, farmers pulled up to the feed plant in a truck and drove away with their feed order.

Macon was a regional distribution center far from everywhere. So most transporting was done by rail. In simplified terms: in the railroad companies' pricing system, when you paid for an incoming shipment, you received a discount if you also had an outgoing shipment. Once I understood the whole thing, I realized that, though verbally inept, the man in charge of transportation was doing an exemplary job.

I put together a report in book form (including a detailed explanation of the complexities of the regional railroad pricing systems) and sent it to the interested parties at corporate. And with the investigative assignment resolved, I continued with my other purchasing responsibilities.

The transportation concerns were not the only ones defused in the early months of my assignment in Macon, Georgia. I quickly learned the prepping I had received about racial segregation was erroneous. The South held great intrigue for my wife and me, and in my off hours, we explored small towns in the area. No one of color ever yielded the sidewalk to me or refrained from using the same water fountains I drank from.

Though Marge did not like relocating regularly, she enjoyed shopping in the new environments. And not once were we waved ahead of African-Americans in front of us in line at a checkout register.

To the contrary, all anticipation of tension related to racial segregation in the Deep South was quickly relieved with actual exposure to the region. I often saw black and white women greet one another heartily with hugs when meeting on the street. That was something I saw little of back home, where people usually did not hug in public. Unlike the transportation issue, I sent no report to correct my superiors' perceptions of the South. Nor did I ever find out where they got those ideas.

But tension was not so easily eliminated from my Macon experience. As soon as the corporate executives were satisfied by the transportation report, a new issue put me between them and my boss at the plant. I was a buyer working under the area buyer, who moved on to a new position. Indicative, perhaps, of a southern attitude of independence from the North, managers at Macon tended to make decisions independent of corporate wishes and knowledge.

Go after what you want.

The Macon plant manager decided whom he wanted to fill the opening and made that known. His decision, however, conflicted with that of the decision-makers at corporate. One day, he called me into his office.

"Well, seems like folks in St. Louis want you in the area buyer job," he said with resentment. "I'd like you to stay with the buyer job. Which one do you want?"

It was a strange question since the area buyer position was a promotion with a significant pay increase. It was also strange to have me make the decision since taking the better position would strain our relationship. But that is what I did. And whether or not it was due to relational strain, the plant manager retired a few months later. I was not glad to see him go, but I was grateful for the excellent rapport I shared with his replacement.

As area buyer, I was in charge of purchasing for Macon and several other plants across southern Georgia. More counties and plants were added to the region during the time I was there until my territory included Florida and nine other plant locations. For the first time, I had people reporting to me—a buyer and a clerical assistant who took care of administrative details. I was responsible for purchasing all of the more than one hundred ingredients for the feed milling and supplies for the processing plants throughout the area.

I was handling commodities trading through brokers on the floor of the Chicago Board of Trade for primary ingredients. Regional ingredients and nutritional additives were procured via direct negotiations with their suppliers. I was twenty-six years old, and Macon, Georgia, felt like a lofty place from which I could see Ralston Purina's entire operational platform.

° ° ° ° ⌾ ° ° ° °

The Macon assignment was profoundly educational in ways that left a general lasting imprint. Two experiences in particular were memorable. The first was another confirmation of my naiveté about racial issues. The second demonstrated that I was also naïve in other ways.

The first experience took place in what you might call the remote south of the Deep South. In my purchasing relationships, I tried to take interest in things beyond the essential job. As area buyer at Macon, I had to travel some throughout the region. Often I met customers in their work environments to better understand their needs.

One of my customers owned three vast plantations in deep southern Georgia. We were riding in his car, driving an impressively long time for being on the same expanse of property. He was showing me his plantations, describing every change in crop or terrain that we passed.

As we drove through a certain area, I saw a sizeable two-story house with numerous black children playing outside. I asked if they were the children of people who worked for him on that plantation.

"No," the man said.

I asked if they were members of families that rented the house from him.

"No," he answered again.

I thought for a moment before asking, "They live in a house on your property rent-free but don't work for you?"

"Yep," the man answered.

"How do they live?" I asked. "It doesn't seem like there are any places of employment way out here."

"They get seed from me and plant and work their own crops."

"You sell seed to them?"

"No, I give it to them."

"Do they pay you for the land, or pay with some of the crops they harvest?"

Take care of people who have taken care of you.

"No."

We were silent for a bit. Then he added, "Now, they don't just eat the produce of the crops they work. Whenever I butcher cattle and hogs for my own family, I make sure to get them plenty of meat for their needs as well."

"You don't charge them for that either?"

"No."

It was quiet again as I waited for the plantation owner to offer more information. But he didn't. I wrestled with whether or not it would be improper to push the matter further. Finally, curiosity got the better of propriety.

"Why?" I asked.

"Some time back," he answered, "their mamas and daddies did quite a bit for mine."

<hr />

The second experience made a very different but equally lasting impression. Some friends invited me to go dove hunting with them at a peanut field. Down the middle of the peanut field was a grass strip. When we arrived at the field, we all walked with our shotguns out to the midpoint of the grass strip. My friends said, "This'll be your spot."

Approach everything with a good sense of humor.

Then they all took up posts around the perimeter of the field and squatted, waiting for the doves. When the doves flew in and descended toward the middle of the peanut field, everyone stood and began firing into the air. A few seconds later, it began raining pellets where I stood. As it turned out, my position was not only in the center of the field, but at the center of some staged humor on the part of my friends. My naiveté aided their stunt, which I fell for without the slightest suspicion.

EIGHT · *Forgiveness*

Before leaving Macon, I was confronted with an eye-opening situation. Its imprint was not merely profound, like the ride I took with my customer across his vast property; nor was it in the least way humorous, like the hunting shenanigans of my friends. It was life changing.

Looking back, it is evident that I married an Iowa girl whose ambition before marrying me was simple: remain an Iowa girl. Settling down on a piece of property near her family and the Iowa of her youth with a farmer who would work the land (or a businessman in a local business) while she kept the home and reared children was the plan. Packing and moving all over the country every few years was not.

Marge was reared by a mother who was four foot, ten inches tall and a father who was a Goliath-sized man by comparison. Her mom's primary occupation was whittling her husband down to her size with the same tongue that had only kindness for everyone else. If he wasn't out in the fields, the man was enduring a barrage of reasons why he should be.

That was the example. And, while our relationship was mostly civil—better in many ways than the example of Marge's parents—I learned that my choice of profession did not meet my wife's approval. In fact, this had been the source of increasing tension.

But that awareness did not prepare me for the day I learned my wife was intimately involved with another man. Not only was it the last thing I expected, it was almost impossible to comprehend. Questions gnawed at me. And while some of the questions had to do with thoughts and emotions related to offense over marital violation, the most difficult ones had to do with matters of the heart. Hurt went to a depth of feelings I was previously unaware of.

My wife has given her heart to another man? She's been intimate with another man?
What does that say about me ... about us?
How did I fail?
How could I be so clueless?

Of course, being pragmatic to a fault, I had plenty of questions of a more practical nature.

What went wrong? Why now? I could almost understand if it had happened earlier, like in Louisville when I was putting in extra evening hours trying to prove myself ... but here? I've been home in the evenings; we've done things together on the weekends ... life seemed pretty stable. Why?
Now what?

I had to make a decision. And she did also. "If being with him is what you want, then go," I told her. She decided she wanted to stay.

The episode was soon relegated to a thing of the past, but we needed closure. One way or the other, we had to move forward in a healthy way. Staying in the relationship while lugging around resentment was no way for anyone to live and not an environment for our son to be raised in. We were good parents. We made a good family. Even as a couple, our relationship had many good aspects.

We decided to stay together and work it out. Nothing would bring the needed closure but forgiveness.

NINE · *Catfish Chow*

The thought that I could see Ralston Purina's entire operations from my area buyer position in Macon was far from accurate and was corrected the moment I arrived at my next new job location, Davenport, Iowa. The official position title was again area buyer. But this was my first visit to the Ralston side of the company—pet food—and my first time on the selling side of merchandising. Another big change was the quintupled number of people answering directly to me. I had ten people on my new staff.

In Davenport, we had a dog food plant and a large canning plant for meaty cat food products famously known by Ralston's catchy Chow for pets branding domain. Cat Chow® was but a toe-in-the-water introduction to the huge product line. However small the beginning, it was an uncommon divisional crossing within the company, and one I knew was a great opportunity.

We also had two grain elevators at the site. Part of my job was to make money off of the grain without processing or transforming it into anything else. Davenport is a river town on the Mississippi. I was to purchase grain from area farmers, collect and store it at our facilities, then sell it, and export it by barge up or down the Mississippi River.

I felt pretty good after selling my first grain contract—fifty thousand bushels of corn—to a company that exported grain overseas. Having negotiated a profitable deal, I hired a crew to load the barge. It was all new to me. And as it turned out, the crew was also inexperienced at loading barges. That's why I was personally overseeing the process.

Attention to detail is critical.

Something wasn't right. In a few passing seconds, I stared at the widening gap between the front of the barge and the dock. No, it was not my imagination. The boat was no longer square to the dock. It took me another instant to recognize what was happening. A knot tied by one of the crew members had loosened. With the speed of the river, the size of the barge, and grain shooting out of the elevator at hundreds of bushels per minute, an instant was an expensive critical measure. Maybe that is why I glanced at my watch before looking at the opening to the barge storage area to confirm the nightmarish reality that the grain was no longer going into it.

Time was of the essence!

That simple fact forced my mind to catch up with my heart, which had already recognized disaster and begun pounding out alarm.

"Hey!" I yelled. But I was muted by the wind coming off the river and the sound of the grain elevator motor.

Frantically waving my arms and pointing at the rope that had come loose at the front of the barge, I tried to get the attention of any crew member handling the loading of the shipment. It was futile. Everyone was inattentive, all assuming there was nothing to do but wait while the loading was completed. Not only were they not paying attention, but it was impossible to get their attention. It was too late to reposition the barge anyway. The current caught the front of the barge and quickly swung it out into the river. As the corn poured directly into the river, I made a dash for the elevator to shut it down.

I looked at my watch when the elevator operator got the machine in his charge to stop spewing grain into the river. Eight minutes had passed from the time the losses began to the time the corn stopped flowing—enough time to feed thousands of bushels of corn to the catfish along Davenport's western banks of the Mississippi. But the chaotic situation was not returned to order until we had gotten a tugboat to reset the barge.

You can convert failure to success.

As I again watched the grain begin pouring into the partially filled hull of the boat, my original enjoyment of bringing a successful transaction to fruition was replaced with a sick feeling of failing. Right under my direct supervision, a sizeable profit had turned into significant loss. I lived with that feeling a few hours and cleared my head of residual agitation before I realized I needed to visit the barge management company.

Yes, I had overseen the loading process. But that didn't relieve the barge's crew of their responsibility to properly tie a knot that held the barge in place, or pay closer attention to the work they were hired to do. I owed it to my company to fight for the value of the lost grain.

I filed a claim, which the barge company honored based on my knowledge of the time parameters of the incident. A reflex of attention to details ingrained in me by the Purina training process had saved the day. I also learned I could survive failure—and even better, convert it into success.

◦ ◦ ◦ ◦ ───▦───◉───▦─── ◦ ◦ ◦ ◦

The timing of the move back to Iowa had been ideal. It was good to be close to home again. It was good for Marge, for our family. But the inevitable opportunity did come—selection for a new more challenging assignment, a promotion, and pay increase. It was time to leave Davenport and move to another state. It did not matter which one. It was not Iowa. Tensions were so high that on one occasion, five-year-old Greg came to me covered with hives. It broke my heart to see our little boy that way, as I know it did Marge's as well. This was not the kind of thing either of us had imagined our lives to hold when we set out on our journey together.

TEN · *Picket Lines, Compassion, And Diplomacy*

In 1973, relocation took us to Bloomington, Illinois. I was twenty-nine and in the first position that I thought of as really huge: director of operations of a soybean processing plant with fifty employees, three shifts a day, seven days a week. I had purchasing, transportation, credit, accounting, and the bottom-line profit responsibilities under my charge. It was the first time that everything I had done to date was put together in one job: purchasing, process, pricing and selling soybeans and soybean products, and also operational control of the plant.

The fact that I had experience running a couple of elevators and had direct merchandising responsibilities in Davenport buffered me against feeling in-over-my-head. But there was no way to disguise the increase of complexities inherent in the new position. The Bloomington plant was comprised of sprawling facilities that made the twenty acres of land holding them feel confining. Contributing to the feeling, metal fencing surrounded the plant activities that processed 20,000 tons of soybeans a month and 250,000 tons a year.

In spite of escalated demands, my thoughts were on innovation and growth: How can we make new products?

Several conversations with the plant superintendent made us direct our attention to the rotex machine, which used fine screening to remove soybean hulls. We experimented with added layers of rotex screens to create finer soybean meal granules and more concentrated protein content. The end product was soybean meal granules finer than sand.

> Think about innovation and growth.

Thinking we were onto something of value, I sent samples for evaluation to the pet food people at my previous job back in Davenport, Iowa. After testing the samples to see if our new product offered any added value to pet food, they responded with an, "Eh, not really."

"Then I'm going to show it to competitors, OK?"

The response was, "Go ahead."

The maker of Gaines dog food, a direct competitor of Ralston, was in Kankakee, Illinois. I decided to send them a sample for testing. They saw great value in the product and bought it from us. Producing a specialty product for a chief competitor was operating way outside the box. But my job was to make money for my company. With a manufacturing cost of one dollar per ton and a sale premium of ten dollars per ton, we were at a 90 percent profit after a bit of internal research and development requiring only some extra screening.

More importantly, making creative decisions and exploring possibilities was a transformative experience. My confidence level was at an all-time high since I'd taken full charge of my new position. It was a pivotal time in my career, demonstrating the effect of added responsibility when it was embraced as opportunity.

As if someone above were once again watching and guiding my career, observing my responses, and taking note of lessons learned, entirely unforeseen charges were added to my job description on the heels of that bit of success. But these were not the kind anyone at the corporate level of "higher up" had any authority over. Not only were they outside of Ralston Purina control, they were of a kind we would surely have avoided if at all possible.

Seemingly overnight, we faced a labor strike. I was forced to bring in managerial operations people from other soybean plants throughout the country to keep the plant running.

Picketing turned into nails covering the plant's gravel drive and other ugly escalations of hostility. Once, as the strike dragged on, I arrived at my office to find a bullet hole in the window. Looking closer I saw the bullet also traveled through the desk chair I normally sat in. It was a chilling wake-up call. This was a serious situation.

The imported help stayed for one week before returning home and being switched out with a new group of substitute plant operators. I was introduced to the role of hospitality services and did everything I could to ensure those giving up their own home for a week to come and help run the plant enjoyed excellent accommodations and treatment.

I will never forget a man of retirement age from Memphis who asked how his services could best be put to use. After learning he had been a foreman, I told him the entire plant needed greasing, knowing he would require no further instruction for the job. Consideration of his age also played a part in the decision. It was one of the least difficult jobs we had. He could move at his own unhurried pace. The man went to work on the project and carried out his duties thoroughly.

The next morning, I received a call from the Howard Johnson Inn where the replacement workers stayed. Members of his carpool couldn't rouse him by knocking on his door, so the hotel management had opened his room. They found him unconscious. At the hospital, it was discovered that the man had a severe stroke.

His family came to be with him. One of his sons was a medical doctor, and I went to the hotel room with him to gather his father's things. He discovered a bottle of blood pressure meds and said, "Dad has not been taking his blood pressure medicine. There's no way he could survive without these."

Take care of people first.

I went to the ICU every day to spend time with the family and to see if I could do anything for them. The family shared a deep Christian faith. And the man's wife made a lasting impression upon me. Even in the midst of her grief she was always gracious. She never cast the slightest suspicion upon me or the company for how we handled her husband's care at work or with his accommodations while staying in Bloomington. The entire family was there in the ICU for ten days until the man passed.

Those ten days were some of the most profoundly trying and educational of my life. I had taken on a job with greater challenges than any I had ever faced. In no way did I imagine reduced production on my watch. Yet there we were with the strike forcing our expectations to change. And I certainly didn't think that, being director of operations under those difficult circumstances, I could afford to devote hours to hospitality or spending time at a hospital with people I barely knew. But life has a way of reshaping "important."

For several years after that, I received a present at Christmas from the wife of the man from Memphis, with whom I'd had one brief conversation. The gift always arrived with a note of thanks for taking good care of her husband and family.

With the strike dragging on, I knew the people it hurt most were the employees who had families to take care of. An attorney had been sent from the St. Louis office to help with labor negotiations, but I was not a fan of his casual approach to ending the strike, getting our employees back to work, and returning the plant to full capacity.

I decided to take on the issue myself and contacted two of my plant employees—highly against protocol, which called for letting the attorney handle everything. The two employees informed me of sticking points in the negotiations that I didn't know about. They had more to do with the union boss flexing his muscles than any substantive breach in labor relations.

With that helpful information, I decided to call the union boss and set up a secret meeting—completely off the map in terms of protocol violation. I wasn't trying to rebel. I was responsible for a lot of livelihoods, a lot of families. That was my motivation.

We met to discuss the issues, and I came away with a few items that would serve as a satisfying victory for my counterpart in the ordeal. Going back to our attorney, I said, "I have a hunch about a few things that might get this thing behind us."

Within a day or two, he made an offer based on those items, and in another few days, the strike was over and everyone was back to work.

No sooner had that issue been resolved when the Environmental Protection Agency called, threatening to shut us down. Some people in the housing complex behind the plant had complained that a film of some sort had covered their cars and homes. They were fairly certain it was a harmful chemical. In response, I bought free car wash vouchers and had a few of my guys put them under the windshield wipers of all the cars in those neighborhoods. The gesture served as momentary appeasement, but before long, I got a new rash of threatening calls from the EPA.

This time it was the billowing white clouds pouring from the stacks of our factory. Neighbors had called the agency, highly concerned once again that they were being poisoned by pollution from our plant.

One day, I decided to walk around the plant and visit the neighborhood that was generating these complaints. As I walked through their streets and looked at our plant, I realized one cause of the residents' concern. The appearance of a processing plant filling the skyline could easily be disconcerting if a person didn't understand what was being processed.

I knew the white clouds were just water vapor formed by the heat in our processing and that the substance on the cars was just soybean dust. But if the residents of nearby neighborhoods didn't know that, I could understand their assuming the worst. Our battle was not against angry irrational people. It was with the uninformed.

I found out when the next neighborhood council meeting was being held and decided to attend. Though I was not warmly welcomed, a dialog began. I explained the activities of the plant and offered educational plant tours to anyone who would like to participate in them. Some board members took us up on the offer. I went back for several more meetings, and before long, I was receiving invitations to join their neighborhood board. The dialog had proven to be valuable to both sides. We stopped hearing from the EPA.

⁕

During the Bloomington years, Marge and I became resigned to the fact that we could not have more children. Our son Greg was approaching ten years old when we decided to adopt. Shortly after hearing from the adoption agency about our place on the waiting list, we heard other news from Marge's doctor. Marge was pregnant. Later that year, she gave birth to our second son, Mike.

Immediately the doctors knew something was wrong with our son. Tests confirmed that Mike was born with a heart defect called aortic stenosis—a narrowing of the aortic valve. This meant that his heart operated at about 50 percent efficiency. Instead of closing tightly, the faulty valve allowed some of the blood to flow back out the way it came in, so the necessary amount of oxygenated blood wasn't pumped throughout his body.

The diagnosis meant Mike would have to undergo surgery for a temporary fix at around seven years old. And hopefully that would get him to adulthood when his heart would be mature enough to handle another surgery that would provide a long-term solution. Otherwise, he had a normal life ahead of him.

A year and a half later, we had our third son, Matt. This time, there were no health surprises. Eleven and a half years younger than his oldest brother, Matt was the final addition to our family.

ELEVEN · *A Big Move*

My career continued to be guided by decision-makers at the corporate offices in St. Louis. And I became more aware that this was under the primary direction of Ed Cordes, the tough-as-nails executive who had taken an interest in me from the beginning. Even if by reciprocal observation from several states away, Ed was a mentor as much as a boss. Watching him, the leader in me grew.

But being on the receiving end of Ed's managerial development strategies did not make things easier. Nor did I get reprieve from the challenges of his demanding nature. In fact, each upward move in the company meant I had less hierarchical buffer between him and me. And the more directly answerable to Ed I became, the tougher he seemed. As a result, I became more and more conscientious about minute details related to budgeting and plant efficiency.

We had an old pickup truck at the Bloomington plant that was about 50 percent reliable. It was only used because of a penny pinching mentality. Often needing mechanical adjustments to keep it going, the vehicle was used by the maintenance staff to pick up supplies from local vendors and to move things from place to place in the large plant. When it broke down within the plant, that was not a big deal. But I was concerned about sending employees out to pick up things from vendors. The pickup was simply not road-worthy.

Deciding we'd suffered enough with the old truck, I called Ed Cordes and told him we needed a reliable truck for the plant. Ed told me to go ahead and buy one. To make sure we were on the same page, I explained why a new truck, not a used truck, was needed. He still approved the purchase.

I researched and found the best value was a new Chevy El Camino. Now, admittedly, an El Camino was a finer ride than a traditional pickup truck. It was more of a collector's car with an open bed in the back than anything in the truck family. But its reputation for lasting dependability is what I was after, and small as it was, the bed of the El Camino was large enough for anything we would haul.

Months later, Ed called and said he would like to meet with me about something—face to face in St. Louis. And more than that, he wanted me to meet him at his home instead of in the corporate offices in the city.

I knew being asked to meet one of the company officers at his home was an unusual honor. It had never come up in my career prior to that. But I had no idea what the meeting was about.

When the day came to travel to St. Louis, I thoughtlessly got into the El Camino and drove it to Ed's home. As I got out of the car, Ed walked up to greet me.

"This is quite a nice vehicle. When did you get this?" he asked.

"Just a few months back," I answered. "This is the pickup truck you authorized us to purchase."

"Pickup truck!" Ed bellowed. "Who in their right mind would call this a pickup truck?"

Answering accusations that I was using the El Camino as a personal car, I assured Ed that I did not take the car home at night, but had a strict checkout policy for its use around the plant. Circling back around to the vehicle's legitimate inclusion under the definition of pickup truck, I assured him that more than groceries could be picked-up by the good-looking car. I even offered to demonstrate or to send him photos of our using the El Camino to haul loads around the plant.

For a bit, it looked as though I might have blown up our meeting. Agitated by what he thought was a frivolous purchase, Ed did not find it easy to wrestle himself away from the topic. But eventually he cooled down, and we went inside and discussed the reason he had called me to St. Louis.

Out of many candidates across the country, Ed had selected me and one other person to participate in an extensive interview process that would determine our next position and location in the company. He explained that we would visit the divisional heads of each of Ralston Purina's product divisions to be interviewed in case any openings were well suited for us.

What he did not say, but I understood, was that the opportunity opened the door for me to move into a new division where I could continue growing beyond the limitations of his direct leadership. I was no longer being groomed by this company officer as one of his many managers. I was being groomed as one of the next generation of upper managerial leaders at Ralston Purina. It was the career version of a father sending his grown son off to college.

The interview process was one of the most exciting passages of my career. After traveling around the country to be interviewed by each divisional leader, I was offered three very attractive positions and had one more interview to go.

The last interview was with the head of the Animal and Poultry Feed Division—the product focus upon which Ralston Purina was originally built. Over the years, the company had grown to be the largest animal feed company in the world. So the division was not only huge, but its significance also remained unmatched. An opportunity to work there offered a wealth of new experience.

The interview went well, and the divisional head expressed a strong interest in bringing me on. But no position would open for nine months. If I was willing to wait that long, the job was mine.

I decided to decline the other three offers and wait the nine months. A call came in just three months. And in 1976, my family headed to Circleville, Ohio, the location of a big feed mill that made products for poultry and livestock.

All former promotions had been somewhat predictable steps of increased responsibility and career opportunity. In two ways, this one was more of a leap. Not only was I crossing a divisional border, moving from soybean processing to the poultry and animal feed division, but also my new position was that of area

Patience can be a virtue.

director of operations. I was thirty-two years old and had become one of the top twenty-five managers in a company of 3,500 employees.

Taking a high management position in a new division, I was well aware of the "Who's this guy and where'd he come from?" sentiments. People worked their entire careers in the feed division for a shot at a job like that. In terms of added responsibilities, the job included directorship of sales over Ohio, West Virginia, western New York, Pennsylvania, eastern Indiana, and part of Virginia. More direct customer relations and quite a bit more travel were also part of the new managerial territory.

TWELVE · *Relationship*

In Ohio, my lifelong connection to horses added another humbling experience. I included my eldest son Greg in my favorite hobby, which gave us something other than fishing, playing catch, and shooting baskets to do together. We had a horse that was initially kept at a stable a couple of miles away—until it convinced me to bring it to live on our property. The convincing had to do with an old nemesis: the horse trailer.

I had not owned the horse very long, not long enough to have developed rapport and trust. On one occasion, we were riding the horse on the property around our home and were ready to take it back to the stable. When we went to load it on the trailer, it would not budge. Greg and I worked on the problem together for quite awhile. I even tied a rope to one side of the trailer for leverage, walked the rope around the back of the horse, and tugged from the other side. The horse had a counter-maneuver for everything I tried.

> Some problems may be solved only by tiresome effort.

I patted the horse on the neck. "We just don't have enough relationship here yet, do we?"

Now, I must admit, if one troublesome spot in handling horses has caused me to consider other hobbies over the years, it's getting horses into trailers.

Normally the whole thing went smoothly, a few seconds and done. If it was a horse I had broken and trained, no problem. But once in awhile, a less familiar horse can refuse to go into the trailer. And when a muscular, thousand-pound beast says "no," coming out victor in the disagreement is challenging to say the least.

The first time this had happened to me, I was in my early teens and was with my buddy Dale Pals at a county fair. Dale and I had hung out since grade school and would eventually marry sisters. But the trailer incident bonded us as friends. For more than two hours, the two of us worked, strategized, and sweated in the hot summer sun together, only to be outsmarted and out-muscled by a rather small horse. Exhausted by the horse's resistance to tight confinement, we finally borrowed a roomy double-wide trailer, which quickly resolved the issue.

Many years later in Ohio, there I was in a similar situation, conceding defeat and having to come up with some other solution. Only that time, it was my son Greg and I, side by side, walking the horse a couple of miles back to its stable.

A company's bottom line is ultimately connected to customer satisfaction. So its primary concern is obvious: "What are my customer's wants and needs?"

This is, after all, what's on the customer's mind. And the more the company owns the customer's concerns, the more it secures its relevance in the marketplace. This kind of relevance consciousness naturally leads to two other questions:

"What is the competition doing with a similar product?"

"Is the customer winning as a result of doing business with our company?"

Those two questions were like prescription lenses through which I viewed my daily work. I was a Ralston Purina guy through and through, and proud to be one. It was, after all, an American institution, as stable as could be, Fortune 500 from decade to decade, the checkerboard logo continuing as one of the top brands on the planet. The culture of quality was inspiring.

Combined with the foundation of values bred into me from my youth, the inspiration made it easy for me to go to work every day with the attitude of an ambassador.

Integrity constantly informed me that I was under agreement to give my best for Ralston Purina every minute on the job. My time, wherever work-related, belonged to the company. Even on a personal level, I could not help but appreciate all the company had put into me.

So "work-related" didn't just mean at work. After putting the boys to bed around nine every evening, I put additional hours into my job from home. Much of that was studious work—preparation. Preparation was the supply stream of confidence. So preparation was a constant priority. The new position as area director of operations brought everything together. In Ohio, I had an opportunity to apply all I had learned to a whole new level of managerial leadership.

I had begun to manage people back in Macon, Georgia, with an assistant buyer and an administrative assistant.

From there, it grew to ten people in Davenport, Iowa. In Bloomington, Illinois, I managed an entire manufacturing plant of fifty people and added the dynamic of shifts—three of them—to cover the twenty-four/seven production. There, I learned how to effectively manage night shift workers without being present.

In Ohio, the challenge was to demonstrate that my skills as an on-site manager would translate to effective management of people in remote locations spread across several states.

The words "management" and "leadership" can have an abstract quality, partly implying decisions sent as orders from someone sitting behind a desk for others to carry out. That perception was corrected in each of my earlier posts with Ralston Purina. I developed an understanding of management and leadership inseparable from the word "relationship." Regardless of title, everything required of me at each station along the way was measurable in quantities—tanks, bushels, tons, railroad cars, time signatures, and dollars amounts. Everything was delivered or received.

Behind every measurement connected to materials and their movements was an agreement. Every agreement was formed in the context of relationship. And every relationship was made of intentional relational investment.

Transactions are executed by people. Whether it was purchasing grain from a local farmer, trading commodities by phone through a broker on the floor of the Chicago Board of Trade, shipping materials across country by rail, selling feed to hog farmers, or working with plant maintenance to develop a more efficient process, every interaction was part of a cultivated relationship with someone. And each someone was critical to the success of each mission.

Take ownership of your customers' concerns.

I was confident that what I brought to the relationship was needed. And I didn't hesitate to acknowledge the "I need you" side of each relationship.

I worked for a company that transformed commodities into various nutritional consumer products. While my new post was in the feed division, the essentials had not changed. Everything was about relationships. But adding regional sales responsibilities spanning six eastern states emphasized the relationship aspect even more. After all, the words "sales" and "relationships" are all but synonymous.

Of course, every relationship is helped when we bring something to it that benefits the other person. That fact could not have been more pronounced than at Ralston Purina. No one else in the industry could touch us when it came to advanced scientific research. We had no peer in terms of perfecting bottom-line economics on the farmer's behalf.

We knew the exact conversion of feed into a pound of beef, or a gallon of milk, or so many eggs. We knew beyond a doubt that customer compliance with product instructions would translate into excellent animal health and precise month-to-month growth in pounds. We knew we had the best products on the market for our customers' animals and that those products assured predictable performance results on the customers' bottom lines. Perfection of the science of animal feed served perfection of the economics. After all, no amount of research investment matters if beneficial results are not there for the customer.

Maintaining a close relationship with the company's scientists, every member of our sales staff knew the nutritional ingredients of our products and how they were formulated to meet specific animal needs at various life stages.

Part of my job was training the sales staff on how to leverage farmer and animal advocacy into long-term relationships. When a relationship is evidently best for both parties, it's a no-brainer. We didn't just close sales. We built relational loyalty. Accomplishing that was key to company growth as well as career advancement within the company. Ohio was a great opportunity. It soon led to an even better one.

Sales and relationships are inseparable.

In 1979, I received a new assignment: area director of operations for the Pacific Northwest. The location was Spokane, Washington. Our oldest boy, Greg, was thirteen, a decade ahead of our middle son, Mike, who had just turned three.

Our youngest, Matt, was one. Getting ready to leave Ohio for Washington, the younger boys were oblivious to the impending change, just as Greg had been in the past. But for Greg, this move was different. He was in eighth grade and had developed good friends over the previous three years. For the first time, moving was a painful experience for him.

I had always gone ahead of each move and researched the area into which we were moving—scouting out opportunities for fun activities, ball teams, things we could do together, and ways to get Greg connected. I did the same with Spokane. But my findings did not comfort or excite him. Leaving behind his friends left him hurting. We had always enjoyed a close relationship, so his pain was my pain. Three days in the car covering two thousand extra-long miles to Spokane could only be described as sad.

THIRTEEN · *The West*

Spokane is in the hill country between the Cascade Mountains and the Bitterroot Range of the Rocky Mountains, just south of the Canadian border. The climate has semi-arid Mediterranean qualities. Regional terrain is unusually lush and fertile—soft loam mixed with volcanic ash. In other hilly parts of the United States, hard clay and rock dominate hillsides eroded by wind and rain. But the Cascades block Spokane from the abundant rainfall and tempered winds famous in western Washington. The bulbous landscape is perfectly suited for agriculture. For this Iowa native, seeing combines working rounded slopes at thirty- or forty-degree angles was a sight to behold.

Spokane was once the home of the Nez Perce Indians—and the breed of horses they developed, the Appaloosa. I had purchased an Appaloosa in Ohio because it was too unruly for its previous owner. Appaloosas became my favorite breed not only because the coloring and stature suited my taste, but I was also gratified that I could successfully train the animal to be a well-mannered, excellent riding horse. One job transfer later, I was in the picturesque land of the breed's birth.

As we arrived in Spokane, I was highly concerned about our son Greg's lingering grief. Finally, I sat down with him to talk about it. I promised that if he wanted, I would fly him back to Circleville, Ohio, the following summer to stay with one of his friends. Then I added the option of flying several of his friends to Spokane, so they could see his new surroundings and hang out together there. It was his choice.

"Really?" he asked.

"Really," I assured him.

The offer had a significant impact. It seemed to take away a sense of hopelessness that he would never see his friends again. He was not entirely consoled, but just enough to be able to get his mind off of Ohio and begin thinking about what he might like about this new place. An excellent athlete, he got involved in high school sports and did very well. More importantly, he made quite a few new friends. Thanks to the new friendships, as the following summer approached, he was no longer interested in my proposal to fly him to Ohio to visit friends there.

Greg made the high school all-star baseball team, which resulted in his opportunity to play in a West Coast select tournament during the summer. The rest of the family went back to Iowa for a long-planned vacation, while I stayed in Washington to be with Greg during the tournament. It was a great experience, and I was glad to see that my son enjoyed living in Spokane.

The other interest we had always shared was horses. Thinking it might be a good time to reestablish the connection, I took Greg with me to look at some Appaloosas and choose one. I was glad he had new friends and sports as a focus, but I thought it was important to maintain our father-son activities as well.

As we looked at the horses, I saw that my son didn't seem too interested. We picked one out, bought it, arranged for its delivery, and headed home. Driving home, I said, "Greg, you don't seem very interested in this. If you're not interested in horses anymore, it's OK."

"You mean it?" he asked.

"Absolutely," I answered. "We'll leave it up to you. From here on out, I'll only involve you in anything to do with horses if you bring it up."

I said this thinking it was just a passing mood, but Greg never brought up horses again. I do not think he has ever gotten on a horse since then. Something I thought he had great interest in turned out to be an activity he only participated in to spend time with his dad. Though the loss of that particular shared activity was a little disappointing to me, I was glad we had the conversation and that Greg was able to communicate his true feelings about horses. It freed him to focus more time on baseball and other sports, his real passion. As he did, I returned to enjoying horse handling the way I had for most of my life: alone. And a couple of months later, my new horse stumbled during training, did a summersault, and landed on my leg, breaking it in two places. Someone else may have been done with horses at that point. Not me. As soon as my leg healed, I was back in the saddle.

· · · · · ◉ · · · ·

As area director of operations—as with my previous position in Ohio—many things about the job were familiar. But others were strikingly different. In fact, some things were not at all like any other place where I had held a position. Most significant was that I was working in a region that had no footprint in America's heartland.

The Pacific Northwest region—Washington, Idaho, California, and Oregon—was not nearly as profitable for Ralston Purina as America's heartland. One reason was a lack of regional facilities. When I arrived, the entire region had only two feed mills. So shipping products hundreds of miles to our customers out West, as opposed to manufacturing them locally, meant huge expenses.

The goal was to expand throughout the West Coast. In order to do so, we needed more regional feed mills using raw materials in that part of the country. This would be a formidable test of my negotiating abilities. Thankfully, I had a team of analysts working with me, evaluating data on properties and facilities.

In one case, I arrived with my small entourage at a rural airport, and our plane taxied to a stop next to a Cargill corporate jet. Cargill was one of our competitors. When the general manager of the feed mill that we were visiting greeted us, he confirmed my guess that Cargill was indeed there to tour the same facility. We ultimately won the bid for the facility and two others over the course of the next two years. We built a larger customer base and increased profitability with the addition of new feed mills in Turlock, California, McMinnville, Oregon, and Woodinville, Washington.

Nearing the three-year mark in Spokane, I received an invitation to a corporate meeting in New Orleans. Everything about the meeting was unusual. It did not have a premise, such as annual budget or annual review. Headed to New Orleans, I wondered what the meeting could be about. The mystery only grew when I had dinner with others on the evening of my arrival, because no one knew what to expect of the meeting.

When it finally started the following morning, it appeared a few dozen managers had been invited from different parts of the country. After some casual introductory remarks, we heard an up-to-date company review. Then we learned that six of us would be selected to work on a project with the help of a team of four. Each small group was to combine efforts to solve a complex managerial problem. We were given two hours to work on the project, and then each group leader would present his group's solution to the problem.

I was chosen as one of the six to lead a group. But leading my group turned out to be as big of a problem as solving the assignment. I was not impressed with the quality of help I received from my four team members. They seemed to be disconnected from the process since they were not selected as group leaders. They lacked commitment to the process; instead they were up and down getting drinks and joking in response to questions I threw at them.

Suddenly the frustrating experience ended with a "Time's up." I wasn't sure which was harder to believe: that the two hours allotted for the project had already passed, or that we had accomplished so little. I was sick over the situation. I would soon be called on to make a presentation, and I was completely unprepared. I truly had no clue as to what I would say.

One by one, the other team leaders were called to the podium to give their presentations. And one by one, they turned up the heat on my stressful situation by giving remarkably lucid, methodically developed strategies to solve the particular problems assigned to them. Finally the last remaining presenter besides me was called.

Even with the benefit of the extra time I had by being the last to present, I couldn't do anything. I was too distracted by the excellent content of each presenter and the miserable comedy of my dilemma. It was a classic case of "deer in the headlights."

The final presenter before me was the best of all—great style, great poise, exceptional solutions. When called on, I was tempted to just stand and admit that I had nothing coherent to present. But I went to the microphone and settled myself to speak. What happened next can only be described as help from heaven.

As I opened my mouth to begin my presentation, a perfectly clear opening statement filled my mind. When I finished that, another thought loaded in, enabling me to continue. This happened repeatedly until I had delivered a talk that rivaled the most thoroughly prepared presentations I had ever given. Everything I needed came to me in the exact sequence needed. Blankness was filled with intelligent articulation

Be open to the Holy Spirit.

time after time. It was a persuasive presentation with a clear directive toward solving the problem as I answered each of the questions in order.

Going back to my seat, I might as well have been walking on air. I had not only been witness to but instrument of the impossible.

Now, I am probably far too stingy with crediting God with extraordinary interventions in my experience. I wish I had more of them to report. I am an overwhelmingly rational man—obsessive about education and preparation. That is how I know I experienced a God-moment in New Orleans. I know when I have knowledge and when I don't. I am not one to "wing it" with balderdash when my head is empty. I am skilled at preparation, not pulling the proverbial rabbit out of the hat—pretending goes against my nature. So there is no question in my mind that what happened among my peers was supplied directly from the Holy Spirit of God. It was better conceived than anything I could have prepared far in advance.

I went back home after the New Orleans meeting puzzled by what had happened. I had never known the Ralston Purina officers to call such an impromptu meeting or conduct such a seemingly random competition. No explanation was ever given for it.

Two weeks later, I received a phone call informing me that I had been chosen to become Ralston Purina's new executive vice president over the western region. I will never be sure because no one ever confirmed it, but the event in New Orleans appeared to have been part of a final decision-making process. Upon accepting the position, I was informed that I was the youngest officer of the company in the history of Ralston Purina. I was one of the five executive leaders answering directly to the CEO. I was heading to St. Louis.

FOURTEEN · *Leading*

I had not anticipated being offered the vice president position. The CEO was followed by only five vice presidents in the company. I thought one of those top five positions was something to shoot for ten years down the road. Only seven years into the animal and poultry feed division, it seemed I had options to gain more experience in that enormous division first. And after only three years in the western region, suddenly I had leaped ahead of all the managers, all of them older than I, and now, answering to me. I was just as surprised as many of my peers.

I tried to go about everything professionally, not displaying any reaction. My focus was to earn the respect and confidence of the people in my charge—fourteen hundred of them. My experience of managing people at multiple remote facilities as an area director of operations had to be applied on a much bigger level now. The western region alone had twenty-three feed mills, nearly one in every state west of the Missouri River.

Improve upon what's already working.

Everyone at the corporate office in St. Louis welcomed my arrival with encouragement and offers of help. In those days, the corporate culture was very IBM-like—suit and tie. It was acceptable to be at your desk working without the suit jacket, but otherwise, we always had to have it on. That standard would loosen in following years, but it was strictly observed when I arrived in St. Louis in 1983. No one was ever seen outside of the office without suit and tie.

At every level of a company—or life, for that matter—there is competition. The executive suite of a Fortune 500 company is no different. "Oh, good, I've arrived" is not a real-life scenario. That's for daydreamers or, perhaps, retirement. But being among the executives running a large company meant being at a new level of performance competition. A regional vice president does not want that region to lag behind others. The vice president over the Soybean Division wants to accomplish more than the preceding officer in that position. While everyone honors platforms of success already in place, no one is there to babysit the status quo. Innovators occupy those offices.

And everyone in the executive office suite is in competition with the competition—the leaders of other companies out there who want to increase their share of the market. I had a strong sense of company identity throughout my career. But in the corporate environment, the sense of our team versus all others in the field was most palpable.

One thing I did not have any inclination toward was reinventing the western region or the role of its vice president. An existing flow of managerial teamwork was already in place. My goal was to improve upon what was already there. My approach to leadership was apparently what got me to St. Louis far ahead of schedule. So there was no reason to change me either. I would apply the leadership I had practiced all along.

° ° ° ° ∘━━━━━◉━━━━━∘ ° ° ° °

My belief about leading—affirmed at every level of earlier managerial experience—began with this: a team is a noble entity of its own. The first cause of leadership is to recognize the team, and second is to identify its mission. These are one and two because a healthy team is served by its leadership.

Identify the team mission.

The most important aspect of a team is its mission. And leadership is best applied in service of the team mission. When the leader demonstrates humility of subordination to the team's mission, others easily adopt and follow this precedent of service. This creates an environment where benevolent leadership is believable. The leader is not there for self-gain or a personal agenda. The leader is there to lead the team toward successfully accomplishing its mission. The atmosphere becomes one of, "This is who we are … this is what we are together to accomplish!" The mission itself is team identity.

I never found it desirable to say, "I accomplished this." Like experiencing a visit to the Grand Canyon with a friend as opposed to being alone, "we" is much more gratifying where breath-taking is concerned. It is the same with teams and accomplishment. For any true team member, it is most meaningful to say, "Look what we accomplished."

The leader's primary role is to create 100 percent buy-in. Belief in the mission is necessary if you're going to follow a leader committed to it. Many outside elements will pull and tug on the commitment. So everyone must believe in the team mission to completely own their role within the context of the team. When facing adversity, unity of conviction and commitment will strengthen team cohesion.

After the task of inspiring 100 percent buy-in, leading is about empowering every member of the team to carry out the mission. Realization of importance produces genuine enthusiasm, which translates into going "above and beyond" for the team. Key team members must feel like entrepreneurs, like they are managing their company. Their area is a business entity of its own.

"Tell me how you would manage this region if it were your own company," I asked in meetings. I wanted my managers to think through every area of their responsibilities with that mentality because I wanted their best qualities of leadership and creativity to emerge. They had to know it was not merely a technique on my part, but sincere.

The leader's role is to create 100% buy-in.

Once we agreed on the policy or approach they came up with, I would not meddle in it or be intrusive. What I wanted from there was to receive reports on progress. Only when progress was lacking would we reassess the approach.

Individual empowerment is inspired one-on-one before it is

ingrained culturally. And it is only possible in an environment of trust, transparency, and integrity. Leaders who exemplify these qualities create success that perpetuates itself in their absence.

Empowering others to cultivate success has become somewhat vogue in recent decades. But it was nearly unheard of in corporate America of the 1970s and '80s. Most leaders back then took the celebrity approach: "Here is my vision, and here are my demands ... what I want accomplished is what's important here."

The celebrity approach is dependent upon personality-driven command and results. The nobility of the team and shared identity with its mission are lost. And overvaluation of one person's role compared to all others is an incubator for overstressed leaders trying to bend their subordinates' activities to their will. More often than not, it includes aggressive, erratic reactions when anything goes awry or goals are not reached.

Observing leader-dominated paradigms reminded me of watching horse handlers using bullying techniques during my youth. Even as a kid, I thought that seemed ridiculous. Sure, it took a little more time to cultivate relationships, but cooperation was worth it.

Maybe that's where the term "horse sense" comes from. Growing up working with horses taught me to develop relational character and honor it with patience and consistency. This fosters trust. Much of my leadership style was ingrained in me before I ever heard of Ralston Purina. But it matured there. Horses aren't the only creatures that appreciate consistency and thrive on trust. While humans don't have 320-degree vision, they are equally offended when blindsided with erratic behavior. And in an office, trust is damaged by offenses to the character of a relationship just as quickly as it is in a corral. On a team, damaged trust turns synergy of power into distraction and struggle.

A leader serves the team mission.

But leadership dedicated to team-wide distribution of empowerment is not some fluffy concept. It is not about milquetoast leadership. I had the title and authority to do what I wanted. I chose to use it to invest in relationships that empowered others. I was happy to be on our team, not just ordering parts on my team.

When necessary, I could be as tough as anyone. Like all other corporate executives, I was driven by bottom-line results. And my goals were not soft. But I accomplished them more efficiently with teammates who shared my commitment. Over time, I learned that achieving a goal did not end leadership responsibilities. When the team accomplished a goal, it was important to celebrate well. Too often, goals are feverishly pursued and reached only to result in the familiar "Next!" announcing the new goal to be pursued.

This mentality is common and inhumane. We are creatures driven by meaning. If something is worth doing, it is worth celebrating when done well. To fall short in that capacity as a leader is to undermine meaning. And sooner or later, that will undermine the ability of team members to believe in a mission and care about identification with the team.

Vice president over the western region was a dream job. I enjoyed the people, the travel, and the things we accomplished as a team. It also worked out well for my family. I worked primarily out of St. Louis, but because I was head of the western region, my family could remain out west. I worked one week a month from Spokane. I also saw my family many other times when business travel took me westward.

Sometime during his junior year of high school, I had promised my son Greg he would not have to move again—that he would graduate high school in Spokane where all of his friends were. I would have fulfilled the promise no matter what. But my position over the western region really made it workable.

After graduating, Greg was off to college. Despite a baseball scholarship offer in Washington, he decided to head to St. Louis with the rest of the family, where he attended the University of Missouri in St. Louis (UMSL). For the first time in my career, no transfer loomed on the three-year horizon. We would be in St. Louis for the next sixteen years.

FIFTEEN · *Negotiating*

Throughout the seventeen years leading to Ralston Purina's corporate offices, Ed Cordes and others made decisions that directed my career path to that ultimate location. Their insights shaped me as a manager and a leader. As an officer of the company, I was entrusted with doing the same for the next generation of managers and leaders. I was not just the team boss but also the team builder.

Negotiating comes down to relationships and give and take.

One of the most important aspects of every position I held over the years was negotiation. It did not matter what the location, what type of manufacturing facility we ran, or what my title was, the ability to negotiate was critical.

Raw materials accounted for 75 percent of the costs that went into our products. Only 15 percent was attributable to manufacturing. Serving the company well meant constantly refining negotiation skills. A big part of my new job was to teach those skills to others.

People involved in purchasing thought of themselves as sophisticated financial thinkers. So negotiating was a natural part of their thinking—or so they thought. But they would miss many details and many dollars by thinking "negotiating" was merely doing thorough research. Negotiating always comes down to relationships and person-to-person give and take, something most people would rather avoid.

Negotiation is a learned skill, refined with practice.

Every region of the United States has different indigenous plant life and minerals, as well as its own climate-appropriate crops. Depending on direction from the scientific staff as to how much of what essential ingredient (i.e. protein) could be supplied by a particular local source (i.e. soybean meal), formulators developed each product regional feed mills would produce. It was up to the local buyer to find sources for the highest quality ingredients and negotiate the best price for each shipment.

Being the sophisticated financial thinkers that they were, buyers often regarded logistics as beneath them (not to mention being more complex than they wanted to deal with). The truth was: it was impossible to have sound purchasing practices without due diligence in something as costly as transportation.

Though using regional feedstock saved on shipping costs, logistical arrangements within a region were still a significant part of the raw materials cost. Those arrangements had to be made with bottom-line sensitivity. Everything had to be negotiated.

At the other end of the transportation issue, logistical specialists did not typically consider themselves as negotiators and resisted playing that role. They were more inclined to think of their task in terms of routing and scheduling. But I taught them to think of the relationship from the perspective of the rail, water, and wheel services doing business with us.

"What does it mean to their business to have us as a client? We are one of the largest purchasers of high volume shipping in the country," I would preach. "Leverage that into the best negotiated price on every shipment. How many thousands of tons of materials are we shipping a month? Always keep that number in mind and think of it as power to negotiate a better price. Negotiate a price from point A to point C, instead of point A to point B to point C. Negotiate based on multiple rail cars of grain, multiple shipments per month. You own a significant piece of the economic pie. Negotiate a win-win for us and the transport company."

> "Win-Win" is the goal of and key to negotiating.

The "win-win" situation is the goal of and the key to skilled negotiating. When understood, it takes the sharp edge, the haggling, and the sleight-of-hand out of this important aspect of doing business. Most people become stressed out about the very idea of negotiating because they assume they are expected to pick the other guy's pocket, or pull off "the deal of the century."

But in healthy negotiating, the deal of the century would actually be historic for how well it benefited all parties involved.

Whether cognizant of it or not, children begin negotiation as soon as they become aware of someone else having something they want—or visa versa. To some extent, we negotiate in every relationship during our lives. But that doesn't mean excellence in negotiating comes naturally. Most people generally get far less than they deserve. That's because getting what we deserve depends on one conviction: We get what we negotiate. And there is no such thing as a born negotiator. It is a learned skill, refined with practice.

Negotiation is the process by which diverse viewpoints come to a point of agreement. It is among the most honorable endeavors. So the ideal starting point of negotiation is mutual presumption of nobility (nothing bogs down negotiations faster than suspicion). I believe people are fundamentally fair and reasonable. This is connected to an even deeper core conviction that we are relational beings. If stated conversationally, this overarching belief defines negotiating in this way:

"Somehow, with all the paths we could have taken, we wound up here together. It must be for the purpose of doing some good for each other."

My counterpart in a deal could always prove me wrong. Projected repute is not naiveté. Rather, it is a high-ground disposition—a place where all things beneath assumed integrity readily appear as they are. The skin of rotten fruit is easily peeled away by a sharp blade—in this case, good questions and astute observation. So I can afford to always begin with a belief in the nobility of negotiating and the nobility of both parties sitting down together to work toward agreement. The situation is ripe with "both-win" potential.

> Begin negotiating with a belief in the nobility of both parties.

That which is unworthy of assumed integrity has a way of being exposed.

I was sitting on one side of the negotiating table with a few members of my team. Across from us, several people represented a German company, one of several sources supplying our feed mills with lysine, a nutritional additive. My counterpart, the lead negotiator for the German company, was a man named Kino.

An animal feed additive of rising importance across the industry at the time, lysine is an amino-acid component of protein. Only a handful of companies in the world produced lysine. We did business with several of them.

"Kino, what kind of a discount can we work out if we give you 15 percent more of our lysine business?" I asked.

With an unusual air of control, Kino said, "We don't want any more of your business. We have 18.2 percent of your business presently, and that is all we want."

I had no reply. In fact, I did everything I could to restrain any reaction—or at least to keep reaction from visibility. Beneath my skin, I had plenty of hot reaction. The idea that a company representative would so boldly reject millions of dollars of business from one of the largest users of lysine in the world was as stunning as it was odd. That Kino knew the precise amount of our lysine business his company had—to a tenth of a percent—was galling. Those details were highly sensitive and guarded. No negotiator would ever allow such a thing to be known.

Even so, using the information to reject business instead of using it as leverage to negotiate more business seemed strange. Something afoul was at work, and knowing that, it was hard for me to remain composed and seated for the rest of the meeting.

Of course, it occurred to me that a member of my own team might have leaked those proprietary details. How else could an outsider have known?

But we operated by the dictum: trust entirely or not at all. I knew our relationships within the team were sound. They were certainly too important to handle carelessly by letting the situation introduce distrust. The first chance I got, I asked everyone with access to that information what they thought of the encounter. Everyone was as puzzled as I.

We soon had answers. Months after the meeting, an international price-fixing cartel—involving all sources of lysine—was exposed. With numerous others, the man who had left me dumbstruck at the negotiating table was headed for time behind bars. He knew exactly how much of our business he had and how much his company wanted because they were in cahoots with their competitors. Sharing information on lysine sales was just a small piece of the conspiracy. It turned out to be one of the largest price-fixing busts in history.

Interestingly, a housewife and mother of three in Moweaqua, Illinois, had forced this into the light. Her name was Ginger Whitacre and her husband was Mark Whitacre, a top executive at Archer Daniels Midland in Decatur, Illinois. ADM was one of the largest names in the agricultural industry. And one of its most important products was lysine.

Though lysine was just one of many things ADM did well, its $300 million Decatur plant was the largest in the world. ADM had a huge prominence in the lysine market.

Shortly after becoming a top officer at ADM, Mark Whitacre was introduced to ADM's cartel activities and became involved with the price-fixing scheme. When he admitted this to his wife, she insisted he turn himself in immediately. Mark knew it was the right thing to do, but told Ginger it would mean losing everything. Ginger did not need time to think about her response: "I would rather be homeless than live in a home supporting criminal activities."

Within hours, FBI members were sitting with the young couple in their splendid home discussing the matter. Beginning with that conversation, Mark courageously endured three years of living every day of his life "wired" (the longest period of time in history that anyone has ever been a wired informant for the FBI). Those efforts led to the breakup of the price-fixing cartel (dramatized in the movie *The Informant*, starring Matt Damon).

Though separated by about fifteen years, Mark Whitacre and I were professional peers. We both enjoyed careers with leading companies in the agricultural industry. And we both rose to executive status in our thirties. We knew each other, respected each another, and did business together.

I had no idea that each time we met for business over a three-year period, every word that came out of my mouth was recorded. Nor did I know of the stresses unrelated to business negotiations that Mark was under in those situations.

Do the right thing.

But looking back, I am glad I did not need to know. When you don't realize you are negotiating with someone who is wired by the FBI, a habit of going about your business with integrity turns out to be a priceless investment.

<hr />

Because negotiating is a process of discovery, it is served by five primary tools: preparation, questions, listening, answers, and patience.

The experienced negotiator enters discussions thoroughly educated on points of leverage and flexibility on both sides. Before the negotiations, he or she anticipates questions and answers and copiously prepares. Then the actual negotiations are served best by listening. The entire process is served by patience, because negotiators appreciate the fact that time is power. All of these factors in balance enable negotiators to convert hindsight into foresight, leading to both sides owning "best" results.

Negotiating is best served by patience.

I never sat down to discuss a potential agreement without determining to accomplish what was in the best interest of Ralston Purina. And as a divisional head, one of my chief responsibilities was to ensure that my team also held this conviction and that its members took pride in being skilled professional negotiators.

One area of negotiation in particular required the constant attention of the members of my managerial team: remote negotiating. Each of them had to know grains and the international grain market. They had to do business on a daily basis in that market with traders all over the world.

And trading with shrewd business people from around the world sharpened their skills. Trading commodities on the international cash and futures market, they had to appreciate the value of an eighth of a cent where it multiplied across hundreds of thousands of bushels of grain. For some, trading in a global marketplace could be exciting—even addicting. But it was not a place for undisciplined enthusiasm. Nor was it suited for the stubborn. Where trading commodities was concerned, those were deadly vices. Successful grain traders are equal parts flexible and astute. Above all, they place a premium on preparation.

From my first post as a buyer at the soybean processing plant in Louisville, Kentucky, commodities trading was one of my primary responsibilities. It required continual education—not only to keep up with changing policies in an industry growing exponentially, but also to keep up with what was going on in the world that affected current commodity pricing.

To understand commodities trading, you should appreciate the significance of the city of Chicago. I was constantly connected to that great city—in particular, to one of its most historic institutions, the Chicago Board of Trade.

SIXTEEN · *Competition*

The wind in Chicago is motivating.

It gathers chill on Lake Michigan before racing into the city to make deliveries up and down busy streets. Rushing through skyscraper corridors designed to funnel its energy, it shoves pedestrians around. Whether in the face or from behind, it inspires people to accelerate the pace to their destinations or at least to places where they can turn and get out of its way.

Off the streets, through revolving doors, moved along by escalators and elevators, competition is an economic accelerator like the wind in the Windy City.

Nowhere in Chicago is competition more heartily demonstrated than in its central business district. With the Chicago River defining its boundaries north and west, Lake Michigan on the east, and Roosevelt Road on the south, locals know the district as the Loop.

If the economic center has a center, it is the Chicago Board of Trade at LaSalle and West Jackson.

The CBOT is the oldest commodities exchange in the world. It is also the number-one commodities exchange in the world, and the leader in the fastest growing international market. A fine-tuned institution, I recall only one time in all my years of association with the CBOT when the opening bell was delayed by unresolved technical issues. On that occasion, resolving a discrepancy from the previous day's trading delayed the action by one hour. Considering the volume of daily trading at the Board of Trade, that is an impressive track record, even to someone whose career was built on efficiency and sweating the details.

Atop the Board of Trade building at 141 West Jackson Boulevard is a thirty-one-foot-tall statue of the Roman Goddess Ceres, symbolizing the exchange's history as an agricultural center. Traders converge on this location from all over the world.

Understanding the word competition in the context of profit margins related to the agricultural industry is key to appreciating the existence of the long-standing institution. The margin is where the cost of raw materials and manufacturing differs favorably from the product price at market. A consciousness of making margin day-to-day is a margin paradigm. Agriculture is an unpredictable industry with a vast, competitive field and a survival-driven margin paradigm. And margins are defined in eighth-of-a-cent increments during trading at the exchange.

Operating at the epicenter of the agricultural industry, Ralston Purina and the Chicago Board of Trade were well acquainted with each other long before I ever heard of either institution. Ralston Purina's many manufacturing and processing facilities depended upon its enormous annual investment in commodities. The company's success depended on complex daily decisions to protect that investment. They were decisions of economic influence. They were decisions with power to keep production flowing in many places, power rooted in the historic heart of Chicago.

As soon as my career with Ralston Purina involved commodities trading, I too was closely connected to the international exchange in the heart of Chicago. No, Chicago was never one of the locations to which I was assigned by my superiors at Ralston Purina. No, I never personally traded commodities from the floor of the Chicago Board of Trade. But the activities there were as relevant to mine as agriculture itself. In terms of locations of continuous significance along my career path, Chicago was second only to St. Louis. And long before my introduction to the Chicago Board of Trade, it seems our paths were destined to intersect.

Know your margin.

SEVENTEEN · *Momentous Times*

By the nineteenth century, my ancestors had made their way from England to a small bit of real estate in southwestern Iowa. As farmers in the midwestern United States, they experienced the ups and downs of a growing but unstable agriculture industry. During the early nineteenth century, that marketplace was a chaotic fend-for-yourself environment ruled by boom-and-bust extremes.

The Chicago Board of Trade came into existence because some businessmen in Chicago thought they had a solution. It was formed in March of 1848 with twenty-five members who saw the need to stabilize the midwestern agricultural industry through a monitored exchange. The first concern of the exchange was establishment of a centralized location for buyers and sellers to gather and make trades. The second was overseeing the integrity and efficiency of standardized commodities markets.

But these were not the only contributors to the international impact of the exchange. Large scale innovation helped pave the way for the success of the CBOT and its revolutionary impact on the agricultural industry.

Nearly a half century earlier, plans had been underway to create a canal that would link the Great Lakes to the Hudson River. In 1825, the plans came to fruition with the opening of what many called the eighth wonder of the world, the Erie Canal. It linked the Hudson River to the two major water systems of the United States: the Great Lakes and the Ohio-Mississippi-Missouri River System. This gave midwestern producers access to eastern markets and beyond, via the Atlantic Ocean.

Chicago was the natural facility linking these systems of trade. And in 1848, one week after the opening of the CBOT, another canal opened: the Illinois and Michigan Canal. By the mid-1850s, the midwestern agriculture industry was largely stabilized, and international markets broadened demand for the products of Midwest farms.

During that same time frame, Chicago's first railroad link was laid. Before long, the city was a hub for ten major rail systems. The farmer's grain not only had a stabilized, growing marketplace, but also new ways of large-volume delivery by water or land.

Visionaries and innovators in their own right, my ancestors approached farming with creativity and ambition, similar to that responsible for the CBOT's success. And they applied ingenuity to solving some of the same logistical and cooperative issues, though on a much smaller scale. One example was the need for a railroad to transport cattle from farms in southwest Iowa to the stockyards in Des Moines. Responding to the need, members of our family built and owned a rail line that served farmers in regions around Winterset and Creston.

I have in my family archives a stockholder's certificate dated June 25, 1907. It designates John Ramsbottom (my great-grandfather) as the proud owner of six shares of stock in Des Moines, Winterset, and Creston Electric Railroad at one hundred dollars per share. He was not just the possessor of the stock value represented on the certificate, but he was also the main organizer of the railroad, the man behind the corporate seal authenticating the document.

This one-track railroad had one purpose. In Des Moines, the railroad connected to a central terminal owned and run by Chicago, Burlington, and Quincy Railroad (CB&Q), one of the largest rail companies in the country at the time. When the cattle were delivered to the Des Moines stockyards, the engine had to be turned around and sent down the same track, back to where it came from. The "switching" was handled by CB&Q at their terminal and became more and more expensive, eventually putting the Ramsbottoms' railroad venture out of business.

But that did not dampen our family's entrepreneurial spirit. Seeing a need to supply water to farmers whose wells had gone dry, a Ramsbottom water distribution service was created. As lawn-keeping came into vogue across the nation, a demand for grass seed and grass seed distribution companies presented my ancestors with opportunity to grow bluegrass and sell the harvested seeds.

I did not come on the scene until 1944. But the family penchant for ingenuity was thoroughly developed long before I joined the super-sized family gatherings. I was born a Ramsbottom, and Ramsbottoms were industrious and disciplined.

Shortly after joining Ralston Purina in my early twenties, while in a training assignment at the company's Iowa Falls plant, I noticed the very large, old map of Iowa in the break room. In the southwestern bottom portion of the state appeared to be a town named Ramsbottom. At closer view, I realized it was actually the location of our old railroad siding. I stared at the map, amazed. It was 1966, and at a job I loved, identification with the family I loved was especially near in that moment.

Looking back, I can see that before life began preparing me for a particular career, people across the generations created a context for my career. And long before I began consciously preparing for successful outcomes within my career, influences were in place that ensured I did not take for granted the necessity of hard work, creativity, and persistence. I am not unusual in this. The so-called "self-made man" gets help from others along the way. If he makes the most of what he has received, it will multiply, and he and others will benefit greatly.

Acknowledge the people who have helped you.

EIGHTEEN · *Risk Management*

Management of risk was not on my radar when I was hired fresh out of college into the management training program at Ralston Purina. But it would turn out to be a part of the training that would retain central importance in every aspect of my career from that time forward.

The term risk management does not imply conservation, but assumes risk is in play. It has to be managed. Risk is in the nature of being in business and a prerequisite to growth. A business strategy for staying put, or merely protecting against failure, is the most at-risk approach of all. I was never given an assignment at Purina with the instruction, "Let's be sure and hold our ground." The goal was always increase—increase quality, increase sales, increase customer service, and increase customer base, all resulting in increased market share. Increase is assertive and expensive.

On the other hand, risk does not suggest irresponsibility. Quite the opposite, well-managed risk is best for the company, the industry, and the consumer. Confidence in forecasting pricing is the key to willingness and ability to take a lower margin position, which protects the consumer against erratic retail costs.

But where large volumes of commodities are concerned, the stakes are higher because the agricultural industry is especially volatile. Weather, disease, natural disasters, politics, and other factors impact the availability and cost of commodities. Doing business in the agriculture industry holds high risk.

◦ ◦ ◦ ◦ ◦ ▬▬▬▬◉▬▬▬▬ ◦ ◦ ◦ ◦ ◦

The Chicago Board of Trade's creation of standardized grain markets and its ability to ship product throughout the country and abroad via one location were revolutionary. But many significant factors remained outside the exchange's control. In 1865, the stage was set for the next revolutionary breakthrough in the commodities marketplace. The world's first standardized "futures" contracts were introduced at the CBOT.

Protecting against failure is not risk management.

Futures were standardized exchange-traded contracts that guaranteed a predetermined price of a commodity to be delivered in the future. Every futures contract specified the quantity and quality of the traded commodity, price per unit, date and method of delivery, the seller delivering the product, and the buyer at the receiving end. The introduction of futures contracts was also the introduction of contract trading. The result was not just a new form of contract, but markets that were parallel to the traditional cash markets.

"Future … like, science fiction?" someone might question.

But futures were not theoretical. They were based on historical supply and demand, current supply and demand, and expected future value of actual commodities. The contracts had to be fulfilled by both parties by the specified date of delivery in the future, or exited by taking an opposite contractual position on the same commodity in the same delivery month.

In other words: the trade for underlying goods was real; without exiting via another contract, the buyer could expect to receive the purchased grain shipment from the seller on the agreed-upon settlement date.

Use of the futures market by commercial buyers and sellers became known as hedging. In simplest terms, a hedge was an offsetting investment—an investment made to offset another potentially risky market position. It was not made to take advantage of a situation.

A livestock feed manufacturer, for example, was not in business to make money off of the futures market. The company's bottom line depended on profits earned because of satisfied customers. Therefore, its use of a hedge when purchasing thousands of bushels of corn for feed production six months away was designed to secure its margins.

Profiting by market movement was someone else's focus.

Aside from the commercial buyers and sellers, futures trading had another party with a vested interest: the speculator. The speculator was not concerned with managing risk, protecting margin, or any involvement with physical commodities. The speculator was there to make a profit by exploiting a favorable movement in the market. Simply put: speculators benefited by volatility; their bliss was market movement.

Because of the mercenary nature of the role, the speculator was the player in the game most readily looked upon with suspicion by outsiders.

But while commercial counterparts were deflecting all the risk, the speculator was absorbing it. The only way the speculator could make a profit was to assume risk. That was what made his participation so vital. Without the speculator, there could never be a guarantee of willing parties on both sides of trading. Where there was an opportunity to make money from an opposite position in a trade, there would be a speculator willing to take it, thereby supplying liquidity to futures trading.

Liquidity was important to the futures market in exactly the way it sounds: flow. Keeping the futures market flowing further stabilized the industry. Stabilization allowed for focus on quality, innovation, and growth. Ultimately the average consumer felt the impact of these in the form of controlled, predictable prices.

With speculators insuring liquidity by taking financial risk and the exchange guaranteeing the performance of each party in a trade, futures added a valuable new dimension to the centralized marketplace. Farmers could be guaranteed a buyer at a certain price for their product in a distant month. Their counterparts in the agricultural industry—the cornflakes manufacturer, elevators, grain processing plants, or feed mills—could be assured of a specific supply at a locked-in price. And speculators could buy and sell futures contracts hoping to turn a profit on favorable price changes. The resulting action was not merely liquid, but heated to a boil.

My introduction to risk management and futures contracts was not until 1966, almost exactly a century after the invention of the futures market. Yet, its function had remained the same. It is the same today. Like the design of the piano or the game of chess, though complex, the design of the futures market is enduringly sound. That is a testament to the genius of its creators. And through the years, the futures market has been served by an underlying rule for which I have great appreciation, one I learned to strive for not only in business environments, but in all relationships.

Transparency.

NINETEEN · *Transparency*

From early on, the focal point of the Chicago Board of Trade was price discovery. The vehicle was an "open outcry" floor trading system. When I first learned of it, the octagonal pit famously associated with that system was itself nearly a century-old institution. The carryings on there had a chaotic, even comical appearance. But they were orderly and precise to an extreme. And their outcomes were serious.

Traders crowded into the octagonal pit, and brokers stood beside phone decks located on its perimeter, awaiting phone calls from clients. After receiving the anticipated numerical instructions, brokers would initiate bargaining. The ensuing frenzy of negotiation was so loud that it was impossible to do business by hearing. So hands flashed communications back and forth in trading-specific sign language. The result was quickly rendered contractual obligations.

Members of the Purina management team were among those placing the calls, getting the broker on the phone, and delivering the instructions. Our connection to the trading pit was the phone deck. And as far as I was concerned, the only phone of greater significance was on a desk in the Oval Office of the White House. There was no margin for error in our communication with the broker.

> There is no margin for error in communication.

As dealing was done, completed trading was hand-marked in real time by ticks (indicating market movement) on wall-size chalkboards around the perimeter of the large open room. I didn't know it at the time, but I came onto the scene at the threshold of a technological revolution. Soon, chalk marks on chalk boards would be replaced by digital displays on giant electronic boards. Shortly thereafter, computers would aid traders on the floor of the exchange with their number crunching.

The exchange was a mixing pot of local, regional, and global economic awareness—past, present, and future. It was real-time publication of what's going on in the world via display-boards, hand-written trading tickets, the vocal buzz of reported intelligence, and explosive trading crescendos. It was an adrenaline charged environment that sizzled as it declared the meaning of "exchange."

A constant flow of information contributed to the daily story in the pit, information that was absorbed and processed and resulted in continuous changes in current and future prices of commodities. Tariffs, embargoes, import bans, wars, protests, floods, fires, droughts, energy availability and costs, weather patterns, farmland availability, and global demand were some of the moving parts in the congested price discovery arena.

The impact on US grain exports from three months of unseasonable rainfall in Argentina was flushed out in monetary interpretation. The transportation strike hindering commodity deliveries made a contractual mark, either by digit, decimal point, or date—and likely by all three.

The pit on the floor of the exchange was where the world came to set predictable, transparent prices on commodities, based on what was going on day to day. It was a place where protection from risk or seizing opportunity came down to speed and timing.

Transparency is not negotiable.

Surrounding the floor of the exchange was an equally dense and equally active gallery of vested parties connected to each trader. They watched every tick on the market boards, processed external information, crunched numbers, and got instructions to their guy in the pit. And the guy in the pit had the intense responsibility to keep split concentration of focus on pit action and associates in the crowded gallery.

Standing next to one another in the pit on Tuesday were the same people who had stood there on Monday. There was no place to hide, and it was not a place for shenanigans. It was toe-to-toe and eyeball-to-eyeball. Trader involvement was trader transparency. Bluffing was for the card table in the back room of the bar down the street. Everyone in the pit did business assuming that every counterpart in every interaction had sound financial backing for everything they were doing. Participants had to stand behind every agreement, even if poor timing meant loss.

Everything was out in the open. Backing out of a trade was a maneuver on display for all to see. Such things resulted in distrust. And in the pit, where actions were reputation, distrust was ruinous. The same held true for those of us doing business through the exchange from remote locations. There was no hiding behind our on-site brokers. Transparency was the one nonnegotiable.

The intense nature of trading commodities reflected complexity and consequence. Large amounts of assets and money were on the line. Decisions were made navigating storms of economic movement—movements that weren't always what they appeared to be.

Anyone who has ever driven a car will recall the first time he or she had to drive in reverse. It was challenging to look out the back window, accelerate, and manage reverse navigation by using one hand on the seat to aid looking behind you and one hand gripping the steering wheel. Backing up requires a combination of actions outside the norm of daily directional processing. Add to this the complications of a trailer swiveling on the ball of a hitch and using side mirrors to back up at varying speeds through busy city streets, and the situation will test even the most experienced professional driver. Managing fast-moving layers of counter-intuitive information is a challenge.

Making decisions about commodities was much like that. Everything was moving quickly, and not necessarily in a way easily interpreted as, "Yes, of course, do this, and we'll go that way, and this will happen."

Looking back, I see that is the thing I was most drawn to about commodities trading and which my superiors at Ralston Purina noticed. I was eager for complex intellectual challenges and the responsibility of insightful decision-making. It appealed to me, not because I was a fast mover or a person endowed with superior intelligence, but because I was driven by confidence in preparedness. Preparation slowed everything down, enabling me to see into the information and calmly make decisions when the real-time velocity of a situation might otherwise have been intimidating.

As a trader, one had to keep an eye on many moving parts. Names and definitions associated with the moving parts were unique to trading vernacular. But everything began with history, current conditions, and expectations. Thorough preparation was indispensable. From there, trading itself changed the market, and traders reacted to change. But whether or not the general reaction indicated an actual end result was a "watch and see" dynamic of its own. Like the driver making movements in reverse by using a mirror, the challenging indicators had counter-intuitive implications.

A good example of this would be a phenomenon called the "basis." Basis is the difference between the local cash price of a commodity and the specific future contract price of the same commodity at any given point in time—or local cash price minus future price equals basis, again at any point in time. Using the futures market to offset positions in the cash market worked because the two markets moved up and down relatively close together, governed by the basis.

A cash market price hovering above that of the futures market was an "over" basis, and cash falling below futures was an "under" basis. If the cash market was under the futures market and the gap between the two narrowed, that was a "strengthening" movement. If cash was over futures and the gap narrowed, it was a "weakening" movement. But whether narrowing or widening of basis was advantageous or not depended upon whether a selling or buying position was being taken. Since basis typically followed historical and seasonal patterns, records were critical to understanding expected basis. Basis history and expectation were useful insights to recognize whether an offer or a bid was "strong" or "weak" compared to expectation.

Every additional piece of information was a challenge of interpretation in some dimension of market movement. Add a revelation about unexpectedly weak export demand in a time of unusually strong yield, attach it to an opening offer, and toss them into a pit full of market-savvy professionals, and you've got an intense situation. Decisions were made in front of everyone. It was not a place for the timid. But if there was any consolation, everyone was in the same situation. And preparation was the great equalizer.

Beginning as a management trainee and representative of Ralston Purina in my twenties, I viewed and approached the Board of Trade as a level playing field, one that offered opportunities to learn and grow in an international business environment. The exchange harbored no secret stashes of information. What was to be known could be known by all. Publications relevant to the exchange activities were available to everyone. Within the community of the exchange, everyone had the same access to everyone else's recorded conduct. I reveled in the sense of common dignity.

With all of its noise, its intensity, its outbursts, and its dynamic characteristics, the exchange was an elegant machine. Whether physically on site or trading from remote locations, as I did, its product was discovery. Its impact throughout the world was a demonstration of discovery's value.

The challenges of trading complexities did not hinder the ascending popularity of the CBOT. Increasingly crowded and competitive, the futures pit was an important mechanism of price discovery based on estimates of current and projected supply and demand. Mathematical processes employed to interpret economic data became efficient algorithmic filters for quick data refinement.

Yes, the popularity of the exchange was partially a result of its success stabilizing the agricultural industry and standardizing its markets. But something was even more quintessential to its growth: listeners. And the true nature of listening.

Listening is caring with the ears. But not with ears alone; listening is caring with the eyes, with all of the senses informing the brain—the intellect. Listening is caring with perceptivity and elasticity. Listening is a sensory, cerebral intake with the purpose of making informed adaptation and giving appropriate response. Most of all, listening is not passive; it is passionate!

A common misconception is that quiet is equal with listening. But a quiet person may appear to listen while actually being skilled at inattentive staring. Staring and hearing are not synonyms. A quiet environment is not necessarily one in which anything is heard. A true listener craves information. But more than that, the listener loves transparency. Where there is transparency, questions are the tools of the trade. The listener processes information, and light finds its way through cracks in information. Listening is essential to preparation. Visionaries are created by listening.

Successful companies like Purina and organizations like the CBOT began as ideas. They were the ideas of visionaries with appetites for listening to news of the world. They cared well. And because of that simple fact, they solved problems; they effected change that affected lives.

Sure, there is money to be made in big business. But those drawn to it by the smell of money are not the best at making money. That is because they lack conviction about solutions deeper than their bank accounts. Conversely, those attracted to the business world for its currency of information and opportunities to contribute lasting solutions to the world thrive by its qualities of transparency.

Like me, many of those who enjoyed success within the ecosystem of the exchange were never seen in a pit or even on the floor. Their passion and craft was preparation—observant, studious, calculating, always listening, always processing information. The information would then become decisions carried out through representatives on the floor.

I have watched commodities trading increase in sophistication over the years, to the point that I am inclined to think of it as science. Technological advancement has been a huge contributor, transforming the trading environment. Introduction of electronic display boards and computers were but precursors to real-time display of twenty-four/seven international electronic trading activities, lessening the need for actual floor trading.

I also saw the beginning of "options" trading—contracts giving bearers the right, but not the obligation, to buy or sell a futures contract within a specific period of time at a specified price.

Options are governed by a complex mathematical regulatory system. A market of their own, options require a separate pit on the floor of the exchange and an added array of hand signals between traders in the options and futures pits. More and more, the exchange has leveraged a broader economic base against local and incidental economic factors.

In the early years of my career, I was connected to the floor of the exchange via telephone and broker. But after becoming the divisional head over Ralston Purina's western region, my connection was less direct. I oversaw the trading work of managers in my region. But my involvement with commodities would soon expand tremendously.

> Managing complexity means mastering lots of information.

STRANGE COINCIDENCE At my first posting at Ralston Purina, I found an old map on the wall that showed the Ramsbottom rail siding. My great grandfather, John Ramsbottom, was one of the founders of Des Moines, Winterset and Creston Electric Railway Company and the owner of this 1907 capital stock certificate.

HORSE TEACHERS From top: That's me, at 11, and Blondie. This is Stinker, but his name should have been Trooper. He once helped me round up fifty head of cattle in a snow storm. The storm created snow drifts that were frozen hard by driving winds and tall enough for the cows to just walk on, right over the fence and out into neighboring open land. We had to get them back to our property where there was shelter, fresh hay, and water that wasn't frozen. Otherwise, they could have died. We did our work in the dark, and when we got back home, I looked at the thermometer, which read twenty degrees below zero.

HUMBLE BEGINNINGS This is our family's homestead and farm near Orient, Iowa.

I Darcy Ferber
will pay the sum
of $20.00 a week begining
June 24, 1961 until due
amount of $140.00 is
paid to Nile Ramsbottom.
If due amount is not
paid in seven weeks
then One horse worth
total amount of
~~~~ motorcycle must
be paid.

witnessed ~ Nile Ramsbottom

YOUNG NEGOTIATOR At sixteen, I wrote my first contract to ensure my friend's return of my motorcycle—or a horse as its replacement. Horse trading helped teach me this skill.

BUDDING ENTREPRENEUR This is my dog Jet and my cool black two-door hard top '57 Ford, which had a T-bird engine and red and white interior. I traded two horses I had trained for that car.

ONE AMONG MANY That's me standing in back, fourth from the right, at Ralston Purina's Buying Training School for management trainees in 1967. The company's training program was the envy of other companies.

OUR FIRST REFINERY West Central Co-op's original continuous flow biodiesel refinery (the tallest building in the photo) cost $12 million to build. My teammate, Myron Danzer, center, and I had the privilege to show off the new plant to Senator Charles Grassley of Iowa, at right, as well as others on the campaign trail.

EXPANSION The board of directors of Western Iowa Energy gathered to break ground for the biodiesel refinery we would build for that company. By the time I stood before other prospective biodiesel plant investment groups, presenting the virtues of biodiesel production was as natural as reciting my own home address. I had presented the case for biodiesel many times to many groups of various sizes and makeups.

HOT TOPIC Renewable energy made our biodiesel refineries a prime target for campaign trail visits by political hopefuls like Senator John McCain in 2008. We were happy to help promote biodiesel.

The Little Co-op That Could

This small town cooperative lures Wall Street with country charm

A traditional Midwest farm supply co-op reinvents itself for the energy age.

Fewer than 100 people live in rural Ralston, Iowa, and there is not a convenience store within 10 miles. Tucked in the center of the state and surrounded by soybean fields, Ralston was never much of a travel hot spot, even for native Iowans.

Biofuels Mecca. But all that changed once the town's local farmer-owned co-op became the king of biodiesel. Today, tiny Ralston is a favorite travel destination of suit-wearing financiers with money to burn. They make the pilgrimage to visit Renewable Energy Group (REG), a pioneering biodiesel business development company that was born out of local farmer-owned West Central Cooperative in Ralston.

Even with the investor risk—after all, biodiesel puts investors at the mercy of not one, but two commodity cycles: agriculture and oil—Wall Street is chomping at the bit to provide capital to alternative fuel producers like REG. Large hedge funds, investment banks and public pension funds have all courted the biodiesel company in the past six months.

Most recently, two venture capital funds, a major food processor and an international trading company offered $100 million in private equity financing to REG, one of the largest equity investments in biodiesel to date (see "Who's Investing in REG?" on page 33). The financing will help boost production of REG's own and third-

Renewable Energy Group President Nile Ramsbottom believes big-time energy sector investors are a good fit with biodiesel plants.

party biodiesel plants to 640 million gallons per year (mgy) from a total of 17 plants by the end of 2009.

"We suddenly are attracting a lot of people who used to just fly over the state of Iowa," says Nile Ramsbottom, REG president and chief operating officer. "It's amazing how well these heavy energy sector investors fit with our business philosophies. These Wall Street executives seem impressed with our biodiesel platform and where we stand with agriculture."

New partners. REG was formed through the combination of West Central's biodiesel business and REG's biodiesel plant construction business, and has produced and sold the fuel for more than 10 years through its predecessor companies.

Today, West Central owns 45% of REG, which is the industry leader of B100 sales and is the only full-service biodiesel company offering a turnkey model—plant construction and management, risk management, raw material procurement and marketing.

All of the 17 REG facilities to be built by 2009 will utilize patented continuous-flow biodiesel production technology featuring water recycling and methanol recovery and be BQ-9000 accredited.

With more than 80% of the production cost of biodiesel tied up in the procurement and transportation of feedstocks, REG made a strategic move to partner with Bunge North America, the world's largest oilseed processor, and E D & F Man Holdings Ltd., a London-based tropical oil, tallow and grease trader. With Bunge and with E D & F Man Holdings, REG expands its transportation and distribution network both domestically and globally.

"Producing high-quality biodiesel is ▶

BREAKTHROUGH This article in the farm magazine *Top Producer* marked a breakthrough in REG's national visibility. Calling REG the King of Biodiesel and Titans of Biofuels, the article began: "A traditional Midwest farm supply co-op reinvents itself for the energy age." The media continued to cover us.

A DREAM COME TRUE Fancy's first show in 2007 was a disaster. She spooked, knocked over pylons, dragged me, broke her headstall, and ran for the exit. Other competitors were scared, and I was mortified. But by the end of the year, Fancy ranked in the top ten nationally in three of the six categories in which we had competed, even though we were amateurs. Once again, perseverance and consistency paid off.

GOING PUBLIC The Renewable Energy Group leadership team rang the bell when the company went public with a successful launch on the NASDAQ stock market in 2012. From left to right: Natalie Lischer, Brad Albin, Gary Haer, Jeff Stroburg, Dan Oh, me, Alicia Clancy, and Dave Elsenbast.

LOVE & FAMILY Business accomplishments are worthy pursuits, but nothing has ever made me prouder than my sons, from left, Matt, Mike, and Greg. My wife, Terry, and I received the "Lightbringer" Award for a variety of services to veterans rendered through our charitable organization, God Cares.

TWENTY · *Going Solo*

Winds of change are, by nature, surprising. They introduce unexpected challenges you can't prepare for. They often come not from the north, south, east, or west, but from "out of nowhere." On other occasions, even seeing them coming, we're left surprised in the disorientation of displacement.

If you handle the winds well, they can grow fond of you and stick around, with change becoming kind of a new normal. That was my experience, and in that order.

Change is the new normal.

In the early 1980s, Ralston Purina reversed its earlier diversification movement and returned to its roots in animal nutrition, concentrating on pet food products.

Continental Baking, Van Camp's seafood products, Keystone Ski Resort in Colorado, and The St. Louis Blues hockey franchise (with its home arena, The Checkerdome) were all sold. Cereal brands were spun off into a new entity, Ralcorp. Purina Mills was set up as a separate corporation focused on the original product line: animal and poultry feed.

As vice president over the western region of the feed division, I was no longer working directly for Ralston Purina. I was with Purina Mills. The changes were huge, but were not initially dramatic alterations. My responsibilities over the western region remained mostly the same. They kept me busy enough to happily leave all the organizational restructuring to others.

But the western region did not keep me insulated from those activities for long.

One day, the CEO of Purina, Dub Jones, came to my office and began talking about the restructured relationship between Ralston Purina and Purina Mills. While Purina Mills was legally independent—with separate legal and accounting—it maintained a subsidiary status subject to Ralston managerial direction. Ralston management wanted to continue that influence, though no longer as a free service—they wanted a fee involved. My boss wanted to see if we could come up with a better idea.

He asked what it might look like if I were to redesign Purina's business infrastructure, and I shared some thoughts that we briefly discussed. Before he left my office, he gave me the task of developing a new master plan for running Purina—one that would mean we would not just survive independently, but thrive. Establishing separate purchasing, transportation, formulation, and pricing systems would be the make-or-break factors of the new plan.

I began with Ralston Purina in 1966. For seventeen years, I had been trained and guided and had grown as a manager in the Purina development culture. Sitting alone in my office, I felt strange—I had just been asked to redesign the company to which I had devoted my entire career. It seemed especially ironic that the path of experience

Ralston Purina mentors had guided me along had prepared me so well for the task.

Purchasing, transportation, formulation, and pricing were the guts of the company structure and profitability. I had been trained in depth in each area.

The Ralston side and the Purina side had differences in all four areas of the infrastructure, and the economics were fundamentally different. Competitive selling price and controlling the margins you make becomes the profit and loss of the company. While both companies focused on animal nutrition products, the difference between retail customers (pet owners) and entrepreneurs in a competitive industry (farmers) was vast. Two different economic philosophies were needed. This warranted a cleaner split.

Commodities were the dominant cost factor on both sides. But that is where similarities ended. Pricing in the pet food line happened once or twice a year, and the selling price was always known. So locking in the cost of commodities was fairly simple.

The situation was totally different with animal and poultry feed. Every mill had one hundred to two hundred products, each with its own complex formulations. All of those were priced on a weekly basis. There was no way to look at the complete economic picture for the year. Market-sensitive pricing had to be right every week.

This presented an immense disparity in how to manage the two companies. One of the primary changes in the new plan had to be developing a new way to manage the markets. The approach would remain conservative, but had to fluidly and intelligently address every week from a new starting point.

On the Purina side, survival depended on a much more intimate connection with our customers. We had to step out and take more risks, fashioning customer-sensitive pricing.

I respected superiors—including board members and shareholders—who wanted answers about "the bottom line." But in my philosophy, that bottom line depended on the real bottom line: customer satisfaction. For Purina Mills, this required a new business model.

I put together the plan and presented it to Dub Jones. We made a few minor adjustments, but he thought it was sound. Next we presented it to the other Purina officers. Once approved, the next step was for Dub and me to present the plan to the CEO of Ralston Purina, Bill Stiritz. We made an appointment and prepared for a meeting we knew would be filled with resistance and tough questions picking apart every detail of the plan. But on the day of the meeting, my boss was too ill to participate. A meeting with the CEO of Ralston was not easy to get on the calendar, so he told me to go it solo.

When I arrived at the meeting, Ralston's CEO came out to meet me. He was not alone. There with him to listen to my presentation was none other than Ed Cordes, my longtime career mentor and Ralston's current vice president of purchasing. They did not know I was there to propose a plan that would change the way they had been running Purina and would sever the two corporate entities. But I was suddenly doubly aware of the fact.

The meeting lasted three hours. I had to maintain a delicate balance between forthrightness and avoiding the appearance of criticizing ideals they had established. They threw at me every difficult question I had anticipated and then some.

Anticipate the questions when you propose something new.

The two veteran leaders did not want to see Ralston give up its vested interest in Purina. But I continually reiterated the essential points of why the plan was a win-win for both sides. The meeting ended as I expected. They did not like the plan. But I ended on a note struck repeatedly throughout the presentation: "We must do some things differently to be closer to the customer."

After several similar meetings, terms were finally reached and the plan was put into effect.

Fresh off of the success, another unexpected challenge awaited me. The CEO of Purina told me, "I have something else I want you to consider very seriously. You designed this plan; I want you to implement it and run it."

Being the head of the western region was a dream job—one I had not held nearly as long as I would have liked. So it was a difficult decision. But I accepted the new position. Suddenly I was vice president of purchasing, transportation, formulation, and pricing.

TWENTY-ONE · *Making It Work*

My first role in the new era of Purina Mills' independence was to choose a new leadership team over purchasing, transportation, formulation, and pricing. That meant hiring people who had been at Ralston Purina for years and asking them to work for me—people who had been in high management when I was coming up through the company, people I saw as demigods of the Ralston Purina universe. And among other things, I was responsible to oversee all of Purina Mills' commodities trading.

It was one thing to design the bold new plan. But suddenly, I had to back that up by making it work.

When it came to trading, the people I wanted on my team had a unique combination of characteristics. At the top of the list was productivity ethic (work ethic with accomplishment-oriented emphasis), followed by integrity, humility, and confidence.

Trading commodities is similar to playing golf. The "gods" of the game don't like overconfidence. In fact, that's a disaster waiting to happen. Grain markets demand understanding. So humility shows in a person's research acumen. Proper humility holds no aspect of due diligence in low regard. Industry is not at all like the giant, impervious, automatically sustainable phenomenon in the back of most peoples' minds. It is not something to take for granted; it's not something we should assume will always be here. Based on pennies-on-the-dollar margins, it's a fragile equilibrium. Proper respect for industry begins with humility as a basis for sound preparation and worthy stewardship.

Humility, then, is directly related to confidence. In all things, preparation is the key to confidence, and confidence is the key to decisiveness. No discipline demonstrates this principle better than trading commodities. Trading, after all, is about making decisions. And every decision is ultimately its own point of boldness. Nevertheless, the markets can be fickle and quickly turn on you. A trader has to be confident enough to live another day when best efforts go bad and leave him feeling like a fool. Humility and confidence ... it's not just a matter of balance; they're inseparable.

Humility and confidence are inseparable.

Numerous people beneath me were designated to make recommendations on commodities purchases. They could trade or buy on their own, but could not trade on the floor of the Chicago Board of Trade. Only four traders could actually trade there. And my goal was to train those trusted to make recommendations to become one of "the four." Each gained expertise in certain commodities, and the team was built so I could act upon their recommendations most of the time.

Preparation is the key to confidence, and confidence is the key to decisiveness.

Trusting my people to research well was essential because it would have been impossible for me or the four traders at the exchange to do all the research ourselves. And to my way of thinking, only a foolish superior would trump the kind of preparation expected of my team based on seniority. They had earned the authority to act independently because they demonstrated adherence to our "block and tackle" fundamentals approach. Nothing was based on "back when I did it this way." Everything constantly changed. Preparation had to be current. We did not allow "trader intuition," and I had no interest in any nonsense about anyone's "intuitive track record." Only insight based on thorough due diligence was acceptable.

Anyone making a recommendation to me could expect questions all the way down to the scientific and formulation level. If these people could tell me what the recommendation was based on, I never second-guessed their decisions. That was their expertise. They were the professionals doing the "math."

But if they could not tell me the process and detailed information behind their decision, we had a problem. Even at eighth-of-cent increments, careless handling of five million tons of commodities a year would be disastrous.

What was at stake was getting undersold in the marketplace by our competitors. But our strategies were not designed to merely avoid something so dubious. Our focus was to optimize margin profitability while maintaining quality of product. We picked our moments and created highly advantageous situations for our company. That's what we were there for, what we were trusted to do.

With 75 percent of our entire cost of doing business wrapped up in commodities, risk management was mission central. Organizational dimensions of expertise and managerial layers of responsibility were designed so that only I answered to the CEO for how that was being handled. I took great pride in the team effort behind the CEO's complete confidence. The fact that he did not have to concern himself with the actions of anyone below me was a team accomplishment.

◦ ◦ ◦ ◦ ▬▬▬◉▬▬▬ ◦ ◦ ◦ ◦

The master plan to sever ties with Ralston had to be created, fought for, and won. And what we created and won was an opportunity to make the most of Purina's unique market positions. We had 10 percent of the feed industry and multi-generational relationships with farmers across the country. The question was: "How can we take customer service a step further and do more as an advocate of the customer?" The new team was built to answer that question and do so in a way that was good for the farmers and for Purina.

Customer satisfaction is the real bottom line.

I began the process with a research project. We met with some long-standing loyal customers in Texas and New Mexico, cattle ranchers who each had several thousand head of cattle.

"What would best serve you?" we asked.

"We're getting older and the next generation is not interested in work that is this hard and involved," they answered. "When we're taking care of our livestock, we don't have time to watch the market and stay on top of weekly pricing. But not doing it leaves us vulnerable in terms of our margins. It's like having two jobs, both running you ragged."

I threw out the suggestion: "What if we come up with a firm price program that fits your feed needs from fall to spring under one price? Guaranteed forward pricing, say, six months fixed?"

"That's the very thing we'd like to see happen," they answered. "That would be a big help."

I had stuck my neck out with the suggestion, not having a plan for how to pull off such a thing. It was not the way the industry worked. Everyone handled commodities based on week-to-week pricing. Purina got ingredients from suppliers, created feed, and in turn, supplied its customers.

I could throw out a price based on an educated guess, but I wouldn't really know what the ingredients would cost Purina over those six months. That could be a disaster. We could not satisfy customer needs in a way that would irresponsibly put Purina at risk. If the program was possible, Purina would also have to get the benefit of forward pricing from its suppliers. Layers of relational commitment were necessary. I returned to St. Louis knowing I would first have to sell my colleagues on the idea.

After garnering company support, the next step was to approach Purina's suppliers. Purina was among the largest users of commodities in the industry, so we had suppliers who valued our business. But giving us fixed-price, six-month contracts on all commodities we purchased from them required them to be willing to absorb some of the potential risk. This is the nature of business, essentially and irreducibly relational, understanding how everyone makes money—suppliers, manufacturers, end-users—everyone in it together and taking no one for granted.

Not all of our suppliers were willing to risk the forward pricing, but some were, including two of our biggest suppliers: Bunge and ED&F Man.

Bunge (pronounced bun´gē, *not* bun´jē) is one of the largest of the international grain processing and trading companies. They supplied us with high protein ingredients like soybean meal and canola meal. ED&F Man, a large international trading and shipping company out of London, supplied another main ingredient: molasses.

I approached meeting with these two industry giants with a double need. I needed them first to hear my plan, and second, to care for my needs as a customer the same way I was trying to care for the cattle ranchers. They had suppliers of their own they would work out something similar with. ED&F Man imported sugar cane as a primary ingredient in molasses. Bunge bought soybeans and canola seed from farmers.

After many meetings working out the details, they committed to the new plan.

Not only did the partnership of ED&F Man and Bunge make it possible for me to go back to the cattle ranchers with the new forward-pricing business model, it became the new model for Purina in other divisions of its feed business. As it turned out, the model gave us a huge advantage in the industry, causing our customer base to significantly grow. No one else at that time offered farmers firm forward pricing on feed supplies. This model continues to be in use at Land-O-Lakes Purina today.

◦ ◦ ◦ ◦ ◦━▸▰▰▰◉▰▰▰◂━ ◦ ◦ ◦ ◦

Obviously, supreme confidence in the brokers at the phone deck on the floor of the Chicago Board of Trade had always been essential. But under the new plan, the stakes were even higher. Our standards were narrow: only the best of the best. As the largest feed company in the world, our commodities volume put us in a position to be discriminating about choosing brokers. And we used four or five brokerage companies to keep everyone's competitive edge at its sharpest.

Two of these in particular are worth mentioning: The Linn Group and Sparks Commodities. I worked closely with both for years. And interestingly, both brokerage firms' notoriety was aided greatly by the same historic event in 1972: The Russian Wheat Deal.

◦ ◦ ◦ ◦ ◦━▸▰▰▰◉▰▰▰◂━ ◦ ◦ ◦ ◦

Anyone with ties to the shipping industry in Port of Duluth-Superior or Port of Chicago from 1972 to 1974 will recall those shipping seasons as a time in which ships were everywhere and sleep was elusive.

Commodities brokers at the Chicago Board of Trade during the same time period share the reflection. Millionaires were born. People worked from six in the morning to midnight and beyond. They were the years following the 1972 grain agreement between the United States and Russia known as "The Russian Wheat Deal." It was by far the largest grain deal between nations to date.

The Cold War between the Soviet Union and the United States was rife for relief of tensions on both sides. The sentiment was captured by the Russian word *razryadka*, literally meaning to disarm a weapon.

But the Russian leader at the time, President Leonid Brezhnev, defined the word in the context of the Cold War as, among other things, "transition to normal, stable relations."

If $700 million in grain sales—246 million bushels of corn, 37 million bushels of soybeans, and 440 million bushels of wheat—could relax tensions, it was formalized by contract early in 1972.

The US initiator of the trade was the United States Department of Agriculture. The intention was to have the sale spread across a three-year period, boosting farm incomes. The Russian motivation was severe winter weather that destroyed much of the Russian grain crops. But the USDA did not fully appreciate the Russian need. Perhaps in a mood of too much relaxation, Russian merchants were granted direct entry to US domestic markets—rather than being limited to US government grain stores, as in the past.

The Russians quickly responded to the opportunity. Soon the entire monetary value of the three-year Russian contractual obligation was spent. The purchasing binge accounted for 25 percent of the US wheat crop between 1972 and 1973.

As reaction to the Russian market invasion spread throughout the US agriculture industry, domestic wheat prices rose dramatically. Farmer income was not just bolstered; it rose by 17 percent during the first quarter of 1973. The USDA was forced to respond by emptying its grain elevators, supplying the market with its stockpiles.

Russian ships heading for Chicago to load grain entered the St. Lawrence Seaway System on September 1, 1972. They were the first of seemingly countless Russian and third-party national vessels to come into the area and load grain destined for Russian ports over the next couple of years.

Of course there were many market impacts—and not all were good. But they were lively, and it was a prosperous time for a lot of people willing to work hard during the three-year surge of business. Some of those were traders who knew their craft and were in the right position at the right time.

<hr />

The late Willard Sparks and his company, Sparks Commodities, already had a solid footing at the Chicago Board of Trade when rumors of a huge trade between the United States and Russia began to stir in early 1972. But there is no way to monetize the impact of being one of the international brokers chosen to engineer the deal. Great negotiators from other countries were involved—from Russia, Germany, France—and Willard was among them. That was a huge honor. From that point on, Willard Sparks was not just a brilliant trader—he was a legend.

And make no mistake: he was brilliant. More than luck had him in the right place at the right time. Willard was the one chosen to help formulate the deal between Russia and the United States for many reasons. Arguably the most intelligent man I have ever known, Willard Sparks could process numbers in a totally unique way. Among the equations flashing through his mind, professional associations were connected. Part gift, part skill, time after time he would arrive at solutions that would help multiple parties—and do so before anyone else had a chance to get started.

Since Willard was one of our brokers, my team members and I spent a fair amount of time discussing trading strategies with him or his associates at Sparks Commodities. But now and then Willard would call to invite me to a seminar he was giving. These events drew traders from all over the world who were eager to hear Willard's every word.

"Hey Nile," he would say in typical upbeat fashion, "I've got an event you'll want to show up at. I'll say a few things I'm pretty sure you'll be interested in."

"This is an exclusive event, isn't it, Willard?" I would ask.

"Oh, yeah, but I'll give you my company badge. You'll be my guest. These folks are coming in mostly from overseas, so no one will recognize you as the Purina guy. You'll be here incognito."

I would arrive at the event eager for whatever Willard had to say in the first ten minutes. Those ten minutes would be worth traveling to wherever the event was held. Willard had a knack for disclosing some bit of off-the-cuff genius to start things off. He never disappointed those of us who knew to expect it. He also had a knack for picking me out of the crowd with a, "Hey Nile, whadaya think about that idea?"

So much for incognito.

More important, I was 100 percent confident in the efforts Willard and his brokers applied to grain trading on behalf of my company. As an added bonus, we enjoyed a good friendship through a couple of decades.

I could say similar things about my friend, Gordon Linn. But our friendship has spanned more than just a couple of decades. Gordy was not an established trader at the time of The Russian Wheat Deal. He had just arrived in Chicago in 1972, barely having enough time to catch his breath before the wild times and eighteen-hour days began. By the time things settled down around '75-'76, he was a fixture at the CBOT.

Gordy and I had met long before all that. Like me, he grew up on an Iowa farm. And he knew the value of asking questions like a country boy—unrelenting until you receive satisfactory answers.

As a manager trainee in Iowa Falls, Iowa, I did business with him and was impressed to meet someone near my age who was a consummate professional. He was working as a cash trader for Midstates Grain, buying corn or soybeans from farmers and selling it to big companies like Ralston Purina.

Gordy wasn't just deft at choosing effective questions. Like Willard Sparks, he had listening skills that seemed to have a sixth-sense attachment. When he left Iowa for Chicago, we stayed in touch. And when the Linn Group emerged from the mayhem of The Russian Wheat Deal, I knew I had another brokerage firm I could trust implicitly to work with my team of traders and me.

Not only did I use Gordy's brokering services, I also employed him and his staff as educators. Every year after I hired a new crop of manager trainees (usually around twenty people fresh out of college), I sent them to Gordy at the Chicago Board of Trade for a few days of training in the world of commodities trading.

From manager trainees to upper management, for the largest animal feed company in the world, commodities were priority one. We used other brokerage firms besides Sparks Commodities and the Linn Group. But they were key to getting things done in Chicago for traders at our corporate offices in St. Louis and for our fifty feed mills throughout the country. We were handling a greater-risk model and sometimes missed with our risk management, but we had about an 80 percent success rate and were gaining in market share by developing a higher level of customer confidence.

Ask questions and then listen.

It was something like an Indy or NASCAR racing team in terms of sophistication, intense competition, and highly coordinated, high-speed, high-demand professionalism. And it was just as thrilling.

Emerging from the shadow of Ralston, Purina Mills had many steps to take in becoming a stable entity of its own. One was finding a seat for sale on the Chicago Board of Trade and buying it. The cost was around $250,000. Having developed our new approach to risk management, I was elected as the named member with voting, buying, and selling rights on the CBOT, though Purina owned the seat.

I was a CBOT member from 1986 through 1995. And one of the more memorable experiences over the course of my membership was being selected for a commission to create a dairy contract.

Because there was no way to trade milk futures, businesses in the dairy industry had no way to protect themselves with forward pricing. But our first job was to find out how many businesses cared about the matter in order to know if a dairy contract was feasible. Was there enough interest on both sides—large producers and users of dairy products—for sustainable liquidity?

The dairy industry had existed for a long time without the aid of futures contracts. So businesses had their established ways of getting things done. They would have to make adjustments. Futures contracts are based on commitment to produce or buy X-amount of product for delivery at a certain place and time and price. Not everyone would welcome the change.

We also had to find out exactly how much milk and cheese production we were looking at. How many users of what percentages of it existed? Who were the actual players—large dairy farmers and companies like Kraft Foods, Pizza Hut, Ben and Jerry's Ice Cream—and how would we address their needs? How would we come up with a standardized unit of sale?

There were many facts to look at, such as the fact that 50 percent of every pizza is cheese. But a dairy contract would depend upon an exact conversion between milk and cheese.

Once all the details were perfected and the dairy contract was established as a legal contract, we knew the assimilation process would be slow. Historically, not all contracts on the CBOT have succeeded. But after a sluggish launch, the dairy contract became stable and strong. It was a team accomplishment in which I was privileged to participate.

TWENTY-TWO · *The Unthinkable*

Purina Mills was disconnected from Ralston Purina. It was no longer associated with many of the products that represented a century of tremendous growth. But it was still Purina Mills—one of the great American success stories, number one producer of animal and poultry feed in the world, a Fortune 500 company launched on the shores of the Mississippi River with its iconic red-and-white checkerboard logo adorning the St. Louis skyline.

But on a Sunday evening in 1986, I received a phone call from my boss, the CEO and President of Purina Mills, Dub Jones, that left me stunned.

"I want you to be at the Chase Park Plaza Hotel in the morning. A group in town wants to buy us."

The orders were followed by a short, awkward silence.

"Who is it?" I asked, moving past my utter disbelief at the idea of Purina being sold.

"British Petroleum."

"They're owned by the United Kingdom. What does a petroleum company from the United Kingdom want with an American feed company?"

"I don't know. Just be there."

I did not sleep one minute that night. If it had been just a decade or two later, at a time when international mergers and buyouts were common, I would have been less shocked—but my shock still would have been great. I had never considered for one second that Purina could be sold. And I couldn't fathom that it could be sold to a foreign entity. Even in retrospect, I'm impressed that the phone call came without the hint of a preceding rumor. I was, after all, one of the company officers.

Beginning that Monday morning and through the following week, the other officers of the company and I met with representatives from BP at the Chase Park Plaza Hotel in St. Louis's Central West End. It turned out that BP was trying to create a global animal nutrition company. They had recently bought Hendrix in Holland, and we were the next of their strategic purchases.

In another large room at the hotel, a BP entourage of technical support was set up. Analysts in that room received a steady flow of information from the primary negotiations. As the meetings rolled on through the week, they constantly crunched numbers associated with every detail. By the end of the week, a deal was basically complete. Purina was no longer American-owned.

But our customers were American farmers, and the BP people understood that. They gave the officers the job of personally calling the Purina customers we each had dealt with over the years. We were to tell them what was going on and why it was good for the company and for them. Part of what they wanted us to convey was that

BP believed in the great products produced by the culture of excellence at Purina Mills. That is why they saw the company as an anchor to their plans of building an international nutrition company.

We learned that the relationships we had all built with our customers over the years mattered.

"Nile, what are you going to do? You staying with the company?" the farmers invariably asked.

"Yes, I'm staying."

"Then we'll stay, too."

Each company officer was questioned this same way time and again. And with few exceptions, each contact revealed the same thing: loyalty to the company that had served the American farmers so well and to the people who had personally cultivated those relationships.

Our competitors did what they could to take advantage of a perceived opportunity, magnifying the significance of our new foreign ownership. But through it all, few customers were lost.

<hr />

Not long after the BP takeover, Purina CEO Dub Jones announced his retirement. The CEO position would soon be open. Ed McMillan—VP of marketing—and I were the two primary candidates. Ed and I had met in 1973 while both of us were working at the Bloomington plant. Ed was the regional marketing manager. He became VP of marketing and moved to St. Louis in 1975, several years before me.

We both had worked closely and tirelessly with BP executives during negotiations, sale, and transition to BP ownership. While we were far from having any kind of ugly competition for the CEO position, we both wanted it. And for various reasons, we both saw the other as the sure favorite to get it.

I turned out to be right. He was chosen.

Though the position went to a friend and a professional I greatly respected, I'd be lying if I said it didn't hurt. I was disappointed. I had tried for the brass ring and missed it.

While Ed McMillan was CEO during those BP years, I had my worst brush with disaster while trading commodities. Due to unusual weather conditions, the corn and soybean markets were on precarious footing in the summer of 1988. I met with Ed and presented what I knew of the situation. Together, we tried to predict where the market would go. As always, we looked at the worst-case scenario as well as the target we thought the market would hit. Then we presented a detailed forecast of possibilities to the CEO of BP.

"Here's where we believe the market will wind up based on these factors. Here's where the market could go if the worst possible turn of events comes into play. And this would be the result."

We made a decision based on the direction we thought things were headed.

Unfortunately, the market went the opposite direction. The worst-case scenario in our report and its predicted outcome happened. It was a multi-million dollar decision—wrong decision—for which we were responsible.

This was a very tense moment in our careers. The saving grace was that although we did not think it would happen, we had predicted the disastrous market turn could happen. Had we only looked at the favorable side and not informed the BP head about the dangers in the situation, one or both of us could have lost our jobs. We survived, I believe, because the disaster that occurred was detailed in our report as a possibility. Once again, preparation mattered.

⁙ ◦ ◦ ◦ ⊶▦▦▦▦◉▦▦▦▦⊷ ◦ ◦ ◦ ⁙

Shortly after acquiring Purina, BP purchased another significant American company: Amoco. And with many other purchases throughout the world, BP quickly became a brand of international prominence. Their animal nutrition subsidiary grew to encompass numerous companies from twenty countries.

For me, a perk of the situation was foreign travel. BP wanted to create a complimentary international vibe between the officers of their many companies. So I enjoyed trips to London, Amsterdam, Brussels, and other European locations.

On one of those trips, I experienced the strangest flashback. A meeting of BP's top one hundred executives in London reminded me of the meeting in New Orleans just before I was made vice president over Purina's western region.

Just as on that previous occasion, meeting organizers announced that attendees would have a problem-solving exercise. Those seated at the various tables—an intentional mix—were the teams. And each team was to cooperate to solve an international business dilemma. Each group's lead representative was to present the group's solution to the assembly.

With me at the table were a Spaniard, a Frenchman, and a German. I was not selected as a team leader, but it seemed to fall on me by default since I was the only person at my table from an English-speaking nation. When I asked for ideas, the German participant offered several good ones. When he was finished, I looked at the Spaniard. He paused and appeared thoughtful.

"I need more time to study the problem," he finally said. And that was the only contribution he made to the team experience.

All eyes moved to the Frenchman, who immediately threw his hands in the air and exclaimed, "I am French; I don't have to have an idea." He marched to the coffee bar and did not return until the exercise was over.

Preparation matters.

For the rest of the time allotted to developing team solutions, the BP executive from Germany and I diligently shared ideas and worked out details.

Looking back on the experience, I can see why BP's plans to build an international nutrition company did not pan out. But not until oil prices dropped to around fifteen dollars a barrel between 1992 and 1993 did the petroleum giant abandon the experiment. Returning to a focus on its primary capital investment, BP sold everything not related to petroleum. After seven years of foreign ownership, Purina Mills was sold to an investment group led by the Houston-based private equity firm, The Sterling Group.

Once again, shortly after the company changed hands, the CEO position came open. And again, without entering any official campaign, during the time of working with the purchasing group, I made every effort to leave a lasting impression about my knowledge and command of the company.

I was one of the five officers of the company who had remained through organizational and executive changes. The company was being run by the model I designed. So while there were no clear front-runners to become the new CEO as had been the case with Ed McMillan and me, I felt I had good reason to anticipate a nod in my favor. But it didn't happen. Once again I fell short.

Though a completely different group made the decision, they gave the same reason: in the purchasing, transportation, formulation, and pricing position, I was already managing the guts of the company, a position too important to pull me away from. It's impossible to know if that was just a conciliatory explanation. But the second miss of the brass ring was much harder than the first. I wanted the position the first time, but did not have my heart set on it. Most likely that was because I did not see myself as the top candidate. I did the second time.

The heightened anticipation made it much more difficult for me to reset my thinking and get back to the previous daily norm when I learned that someone else would be the new CEO. But I did reset my thinking. It was my job, a job I had enjoyed immensely before setting my sights on the CEO position. It was time to get back to that.

TWENTY-THREE · *Lose-Lose*

Expectations for the future never made it into conversations between Marge and me when we were dating because there was no thinking going on then, just reacting. Why we never discussed something as important as future plans during our early years of marriage is less clear. We shared modest intentions of prospering and happiness. But we never talked about the specifics of our personal dreams, of how such things could happen, or what they might look like.

Maybe we were just too busy with day-to-day responsibilities. Maybe our interests and ideas were so different that they failed to connect enough to stir up the topic. Maybe we both assumed agreement on the matter and saw no reason to bring it up. Whatever the reason, we never discussed the subject of what our life together might look like after I graduated from college.

Marge had three siblings. Only one went to college, a brother who earned a teaching degree and then took a teaching position near the town of Macksburg where they grew up. Marge might have anticipated I would do the same with my business degree—move back to the hometown area and take a job in a local business. Though I had no vision for a career that would move us all over the country, my ambitions were not confined to southern Iowa. I suspect she would say in retrospect that was a detail she should not have overlooked when deciding to marry me.

Accept the obvious, and deal with it.

After taking the job with Ralston Purina, my training assignment in Iowa Falls worked out well for both of us. I was in a position I loved and a career I was challenged by, and Marge was in Iowa, just 120 miles from family and friends back in Macksburg.

The situation was misleading. My Purina career would not include another assignment nearly as close to our hometown as Iowa Falls, Iowa. In fact, only once among the many moves that followed would an assignment bring us back to our home state.

Besides the geographical issues, the biggest struggle we faced was that I loved my career and Marge despised it. I saw the work we did at Purina as noble. Supplying the highest quality animal feed to farmers throughout the United States affected everyone; it was a key part in feeding people in this country and throughout the world. But I dared not share my enthusiasm. It only added to my wife's resentment. The necessity of greater social interaction—entertaining and hospitality as I grew with the company—exacerbated the issue. And as the years went on, the need to defend my company and career choice was constant.

It is not hard to understand the challenges from Marge's side. She never dreamed that marrying me could lead to being a hostage in a life she didn't enjoy. She had to live where she did not want to live and away from back-home relations of great importance to her. And she had to live with someone who was thriving in the very situation that she found completely unappealing.

We both wanted to provide a stable home and family foundation for our three sons. And we both were raised with a solid Midwestern—"keep at it and don't give up on your commitments"—work ethic. These had become the default basis for our dogged determination to stay together. We worked and we worked. But we could find no solution that worked.

By the time our sons were grown and out of the house, the years of bouncing around the country were long in the past. Marge and I had been settled in St. Louis for numerous years with no anticipation of relocation. Financial rewards that had steadily increased from the day of our introduction to Purina were especially good. It seemed like our marriage should be peaceful and enjoyable. It wasn't.

I was never one to engage in combative verbal encounters, but I could deflect or absorb them. And I was less and less able to deflect the obvious: I was the reason for my wife's misery, and she made me miserable for it. We went to counseling, which confirmed the obvious but supplied no balance of encouragement of turning things around. When hope was gone, resigning ourselves to ongoing misery made no sense.

No one gets married to fail at marriage. So no one wins in a divorce. It's a negotiated outcome that is always lose-lose. When you have tried to get something right for over three decades, any relief gained by conceding defeat is equaled by disappointment.

Nevertheless, I approached Marge about the subject, and we agreed it was necessary. Our divorce was finalized in 1997.

TWENTY-FOUR · *Terry*

My secretary, Annie, decided that I had been alone and losing weight long enough. She tried many times to recommend her sister as the solution to my sad state. When that did not work, she was still confident in her Cupid-playing skills. She suggested a colleague named Terry.

My agreeing that Terry was a "nice enough person" did not get the message across to Annie that I was not in a hurry to fix my alone situation. Undeterred, Annie frequently shared ideas about Terry and me getting together.

Terry had joined Ralston Purina twenty-five years earlier and had been with the Purina Feed Division far longer than I had. Her background was in accounting, but her expertise at Purina was deciphering what the numbers actually meant. This was an invaluable skill when applied to commodities.

I met Terry a few years before Annie mentioned her, when she was assigned to an accounting team for one of my projects. She was intensely work-driven.

When I finally decided to take Annie's suggestion and meet with Terry outside of work, I invited her to attend a tennis match involving the St. Louis Aces of World Team Tennis.

As it turned out, conversation could not have been easier. We had many things in common, including raising three sons. We both were professionals who loved Purina and enjoyed talking about work.

The more I learned about Terry, the more I came to think of her as "The Can-Do Girl." She had often found herself in circumstances that appeared over her head. But she responded with determination to overcome whatever she faced. Backing down was just not an option for her. Consequently, she was independent and content to focus on raising her sons the way she knew best: solo.

Even our friendship was something she wanted to remain unchanged. It had its well-ordered place in her life, and she was not inclined to risk that with any definition beyond friendship.

But as the friendship grew, our time together became more of a priority. At some point, we acknowledged that spending time together as friends was really dating. It was a relief to admit—perhaps mainly to myself—that I found Terry to be extraordinary and had developed romantic feelings for her. After almost a year of official dating, we married in November 1998.

> Everyone needs friends.

Another life-changing development occurred in 1998. Purina Mills was purchased by Koch Industries, a company run by two billionaire brothers whose wealth and expertise were petroleum-based.

During the first year, they wasted no time dismissing officers of Purina inherited via the purchase. They moved my division to Wichita, Kansas. I agreed to go there and see my team through the transition. Because of the parallel timing of the move and our marriage, Terry and I set up our first home together in Wichita. But my employment under Koch Industries was brief.

In 1999, I found myself in that dreaded no-man's-land of age fifty-five, over-qualified, and unemployed. With my thirty-three-year Purina career suddenly concluded, I was facing trying times ahead. And I couldn't have had a truer friend than Terry to help me through them.

TWENTY-FIVE · *Back to My Roots*

Being jobless was an entirely new territory. Growing up on the family farm provided me with built-in employment until the job with the printing company got me through the college years. From there, I went straight to a thirty-three-year career with Purina. I had never been unemployed.

I set out to look for new employment without a clue about where to begin. But I went about it as if I still had a job. I got up at the same time, kept the same schedule, and worked as though it were a profession—research, preparation, and execution. I also had no idea what to expect.

One thing I did not expect, however, was a cold response to my depth of managerial experience. But that is precisely what I got.

Most human resource department searches focus on young, inexpensive manager trainees hungry for opportunity. Mere mention of my previous salary was enough to scare away potential suitors. The opportunities that came my way were in the form of job offers that meant returning to career beginnings—an entry-level position and a similarly nostalgic pay grade. The post-Purina reality was shocking and humbling, an experience that somehow inspired my determination to win.

The job search led back to my roots: Iowa and agriculture. My mother was still in Iowa, and I wanted to be near her in her later years. I found a farmers co-op with an upper managerial position open … or two (they weren't quite sure). Their wish list of skills and expertise was impressive. They were looking for someone with experience of a national scope in risk management—buying and selling commodities. The person had to be an experienced manager, able to manage the entire production cycle and national sales of the company's dairy division and two main products: Soy Plus and Soy Chlor. And they wanted someone who could manage their feed division—hogs and cattle.

My experience over many years at Purina had supplied all the right qualifications for the position. The company was West Central Cooperative. The pay cut would be 30 percent of my former salary (a generous offer relative to the results of my job search).

After what I thought was a solid interview, I was told someone would get back to me by Monday of the next week. Monday came and went. A week later, I was getting worked up. I had been at the job search for months and made every effort to maintain a good attitude. I had made it a point not to visit subjects not yet resolved—like, *Why am I out of a job at fifty-five anyway? For thirty-three years, I gave my all to a company I thought of as family, identity, and future!*

> Treat a job search as a job.

But the latest insult seemed too much—*Why am I, former officer of a Fortune 500 company, being stiffed by a little country co-op for which I'm willing to take a huge pay reduction?*

On a day when I had abandoned my job search routine, the questions were flooding my mind, and I was focusing quite a lot on the proportions of my disgruntlement. Suddenly I was spoken to ... not audibly, but clearly.

"Get back to work. Trust me with what is out of your control. Your work right now is looking for a job. That's your job. I'll take care of mine."

I immediately returned to my job hunting and got my mind off of complaining. The next day I heard from West Central. I was once again employed.

○ ○ ○ ○─▰▰▰▰▰◉▰▰▰▰▰─○ ○ ○ ○

Relationships matter.

Years earlier, I had left home for college as a young man looking to distance myself from agriculture and make my way in business. I had accomplished one, but, thankfully, not the other. In fact, my agricultural background continued to be the foundation to fulfillment of that original dream of a career in business. How could I have known that agricultural foundations would lead to something as sophisticated as risk management? This expertise once again proved to be the key to landing a new position I enjoyed.

We created national and international accounts for Soy Plus and Soy Chlor and increased the dairy volume by 50 percent in just a few years.

Equally important, I developed a great working relationship with someone who would play a large role in successes to come—Myron Danzer. The relationship brought into play another of the skills developed at Purina: recognizing talent and character.

Myron was the production manager at West Central's soybean processing plant. We shared some similarities. Like me, Myron was farm-raised in Iowa, was a hard worker, and had a high common sense IQ as well as a likeable down-to-earth manner.

We were also quite different. Myron was two decades my junior, a local guy with no formal education, and he had an uncommon mechanical aptitude.

I was the college-educated manager from Purina's executive suite. (Myron once expressed relief at the discovery I was not a "suit" who never gets his hands dirty and was not the "ivory tower guy" he was concerned West Central had hired.)

When I was a year into the new job, our co-op community was unexpectedly rocked. Doug Stidham, the man who'd hired me, died of a heart attack at the age of forty-two. I was asked to take his position—executive vice president of feed and nutrition—and became Myron's boss and mentor.

In feed milling, we dealt with mixers, pellet mills, bagging equipment, conveyors, and dry-solid handling equipment. In soy processing, there was cleaning equipment, heating equipment, and pressing equipment. Technological issues in the soy production plant often caused Myron, who oversaw all mechanical operations, some frustration. Sometimes they wore down his determination (not an easy thing to do).

Rather than avoid me, Myron would find his way to my office wearing a look of doubt in his ability to come up with a solution.

"I don't know, Nile. I can't figure it out."

"Keep working at it. You'll get it. You always do, Myron," I'd say. The next time I'd see him, he would be all smiles—problem solved.

Employees and the financials of the plant operation also had to be managed, two areas of responsibility not in the center of Myron's radar. These were opportunities for me to be a coach and educator. Throughout my career, when I met someone I believed in, someone whose effort, character, and skills inspired investment, I felt a moral obligation to help that person reach his or her full potential as a professional.

It was fun to watch Myron grow under such tutelage into a complete manager, handling people and financials with the same proficiency he applied to facilities. From production manager, he grew into a first-rate general manager, eventually overseeing all aspects of plant operations.

Help others reach their full potential.

My first responsibility, however, was not mentoring, but working on markets and production efficiency—managing the margins for profitability. The challenge is always to create an integrated sales and production team, thereby making both more successful.

West Central entrusted me with its company growth. It was my job to inspire and educate everyone until each person took ownership of being part of a cohesive team. When a sales person comes to production seeking to achieve a particular item to please a customer and everyone on the production side takes personal interest in that objective, that's when we can look at one another with a sense of shared identity. And that is the beginning of a unified will to thrive.

It was rewarding to see team results at West Central mimic those I experienced at a Fortune 500 company.

One day I was approached by Jeff Stroburg, the CEO of West Central. After he expressed how pleased he was with my impact on the company, he said, "We have this plant ... methyl ester production. Why don't you give it a look and see what you can do with that?"

Jeff Stroburg was a dream boss. He was confident without being imposing. He placed a lot of confidence in me and gave me a lot of room to fail or succeed. Extremely knowledgeable on many fronts, he was masterful with questions, helping flesh out ideas and fashion vision. He was the kind of boss whose leadership can inspire something unusual to happen, something great ... something revolutionary.

I walked through the plant with Myron. It existed as the result of an idea to use soybean oil for secondary product revenues. During processing for West Central's signature product, Soy Plus, oil was squeezed out of the soybeans. The oil was purified at the plant and then sold as crude oil to customers who would refine it into cooking oil.

In an effort to add value to the oil and make it into something other than cooking oil (which was overabundant in the market), the oil was used in smaller amounts for surfactants (basically soaps) and methyl ester products. Initially these were lubricants, like WD-40, solvents, paint remover, asphalt release (which keeps asphalt from sticking to metal), and cleaners.

Crop oils could also be made at the small plant. When they were mixed with water and a herbicide, the herbicide would stick better to the leaves of plants.

All of those products had one marketing appeal in common: they were bio-based, which means eco-friendly—causing no harm to the environment when washed off into the soil.

On the down side: making the methyl ester products required a fairly involved process that saw little profit. West Central needed to move in another direction if possible. As Myron and I assessed the small plant, we started talking about biodiesel.

The nature of our work had been running feed mill operations and soybean processing. The invitation to look into the methyl ester plant and figure out what more could be done with it intrigued me. I had always wanted to do something special, to accomplish something different. If presented with the right opportunity, I believed I could. I really had no idea of what I was getting into with an old methyl ester plant, but I had a feeling about it ...

TWENTY-SIX · *Questions*

"Why biodiesel?"

Efforts to become educated on biodiesel made me feel like a curious kid with an endless supply of questions. But because my involvement had to do with the bottom line (having inherent profit and loss implications), my questions all began with this very simple one: "Biodiesel?"

Initially, getting away from losing money on small quantities of retail solvents and finding a bulk product focus for the plant was the internal answer to the question. Externally, a one-word answer had growing significance in the world: renewable.

The push was strong in the late 1990s to improve the environment, especially to clean up vehicle emissions and get away from dependence on fossil fuels. The government created the Renewable Fuel Standard, requiring petroleum companies to use renewable fuels in their products. So that was the beginning point—the reason biodiesel was a topic of conversation at all. "Why biodiesel?" It is a renewable fuel source.

Petroleum only seems to be in endless supply. While we don't know how much of it exists, we do know it is a fairly static resource. Unless new technology comes along, a certain amount of it exists, and that's it. Conversely, renewable fuels are based on some sort of feedstock, something producible, something that is grown and supplied cyclically, or seasonally. Biodiesel is one of those.

My education also turned up interesting facts that were not so obvious but equally important. Biodiesel has a naturally occurring oxygen component in its chemical makeup, so it runs cleaner than regular diesel gasoline. But diesel engines do not need any technological adjustment to be able to run on it. As long as the biodiesel fuel is pure (able to go through a two-micron filter), there is no difference in its use in engines.

And most intriguing to me was learning that creation of biodiesel is not a high-heat process. The ratio of energy used to produce the final product versus energy supplied by the final product is one-to-five. That is, only one unit of energy is used to create five units of energy! (Ethanol and petroleum require high-heat production and have a one-to-one energy ratio.)

Five to one was a key factor. From the moment I learned it, that fact never left my mind. It was like a first reason to exist as a business entity working with biodiesel. It meant there was one sure aspect of all this that I knew was good for America.

> Learn as much as you can about your discipline.

Before me was an opportunity to do something good for industry and for humanity. And there was an efficiency factor that suggested potential viability. After all the unexpected career twists and turns and the humbling adjustments, after all the undesired changes, here was one that I welcomed.

That is not to say it was comfortable. The apparent opportunity was not without its challenges. It would require a double sale to get any momentum going at all. Consumers would have to be sold on the idea that using biodiesel was beneficial, and large oil companies like BP, Exxon-Mobil, and Shell had to be sold on its value so consumers had a place to get it.

Then there was the actual production side of the equation. There was no point in selling anyone on something we could not actually create at a guaranteed industry standard or in amounts worthy of creating a demand.

Industry based on petroleum byproducts ranged from blacktop that gets spread on parking lots to jet fuel. The renewable fuel products being produced at West Central's little methyl ester plant were closer to the blacktop end of the spectrum. Biodiesel that consumers would trust to run their engines and large oil companies would be willing to distribute would have to be closer to the jet fuel end. The plant needed a conversion of that magnitude. And it would barely be a starting point.

Ultimately, the economics of the operation would make or break our hope of turning the plant into a biodiesel producer. Economic questions always begin with motivation to make people's lives better. "What do you need? What do you want? What's your biggest obstacle? What's your biggest expense? How can we help you?"

These are tied to what is possible. In our case: How much biodiesel could the plant produce at full capacity and at what cost? How much could we sell it for and make a profit? Would there be enough soybean oil (or other feed stock) to keep up with demand if we created it?

But answers to all those questions would not be on the radar until we knew much more about how to get there from where we were.

Increasing dairy volume by 50 percent was a success story I already had to my credit. So I had the confidence of the West Central board of directors as a bit of "leash" to work with. The old methyl ester plant was sitting there, available for use.

Three things would let us know if we should bother going any further. We needed to know if we had a useful product. We needed to know our cost per gallon to produce it. And we needed to know if we had customers.

Thanks to Myron Danzer and another common sense country boy, Matt Schultes, the plant was soon converted to produce biodiesel, or to find out that we could indeed make the stuff. We used it in West Central's diesel vehicles, so we knew it worked.

Before long, we confirmed our ability to consistently make a product that met the industry standard for diesel fuel. However, it cost us a dollar more per gallon to make than the price regular diesel sold for at the pumps. Despite our tries, we could not budge that number.

Solving that problem would have to wait. It was time to move on to the question of consumer interest.

Farms are diesel-driven. Tractors, combines, trucks, and many larger pickups have diesel engines. There is not a lot to do in Iowa during the winter. So in the winter months of 2000 and 2001, Gary Haer (our only salesman), Myron Danzer, and I made appointments with as many Iowa farmers as possible. We met with them in Kiwanis Clubs, Chambers of Commerce, Rotary Clubs, and Lions Clubs all over the state. We went to numerous meetings in church basements.

A leader must inspire and teach.

Our goal was to answer the most important question of all: "Do we have customers?"

To do so, the three of us would head in different directions for meetings throughout the state. We were willing to meet anywhere with anyone in agriculture who would meet with us.

Four hundred farmers made up the West Central Co-op. They all grew soybeans. This fact was the only hope we had of successfully promoting our new product. We could take their product, process the soybeans, and use the soybean oil in biodiesel. It would be self-serving for the farmers (who were co-op shareholders) to advance a product created from their own crops while they helped launch a new West Central revenue stream.

Iowa economics are farmer-centric. The farm income supports local merchants such as the hardware store. Bankers have deep vested interests in farmers as business owners, too. What is good for the farmer is good for them. So the meetings were like community gatherings.

With little else competing for everyone's attention, events were well attended. Iowans everywhere were being educated in the virtues of biodiesel. My message was always the same, not complicated, and focused on a few key points.

The dialogue was generally lively:

"This is cleaner fuel," I would always begin. "That means better for the environment. That's the first thing you need to consider. Secondly, we'll take soybeans you grow and use them to make biodiesel. It will raise the price of your crops by increasing demand. And you raise the value of the biodiesel made by your co-op by using it in your tractors and combines. Thirdly, it reduces dependence on foreign oil, in some cases supplied by parties who are hostile to Americans."

The first question I was asked was always: "How much will this increase in demand raise the price of our crops?"

"Well, I don't know exactly," I always answered. "We have to create demand before we can see how big it is and what its effect will be. I can give you an estimate. I can tell you that creating more demand has to help. You're the owners of this co-op. I'm trying to help you grow your business. Right now this soybean oil has a low price for refining it and selling it to someone else to turn it into WD-40, or salad dressing, or cooking oil, which, as you all know, is a saturated market. We want to create value for you."

The next question they'd ask: "You might be causing big problems for us. Combines and tractors are expensive. Using a non-spec diesel gas in those engines might nullify the warranty. Then what? What if something goes wrong; you going to buy us

Do you have a
useful product?

What is your cost
to produce it?

Can you get
customers?

new engines?"

"Yes. If that happens we'll buy you new engines. Of course, I can only make you that guarantee because that's how confident I am that no such thing will happen. We can show you the chemical constitution of the biodiesel ... its pure diesel! We use it in all of our own vehicles, and they also have expensive engines."

"What's the fuel cost?"

"Right now you would pay a premium for it—around a dollar per gallon above your present fuel costs."

"Whoa, there partner. We might be willing to go with a slight premium to see the value of our crops raised. But we can't go way out there with you."

"No, I didn't think so. And I wouldn't expect you to. Nor would I expect you to switch entirely over to biodiesel. But would you consider using a two percent mixture? Keep using 98 percent of the diesel fuel you've been using all along. Add just two percent of our biodiesel. Two percent of a dollar ... that's just two cents a gallon. Would you be willing to pay us two cents a gallon to help get the volume up and see if we can make this work? Because that's what it's going to take. We have to get the volume up to make a difference in the value of your soybean crops ... say, four to five cents a bushel difference."

"Where do we get the stuff?" was always in the third line of questioning. "I don't know anyone carrying it. Farming season's busy. I can't drive all over creation for a couple-percent of my fuel."

"You leave that up to us. We'll get the fuel to where it's convenient for you. You're our owners and our customers. We'll treat you right. Look, all I'm asking you to do is use it in your vehicles and help create demand that will raise the value of your company products in two ways.

"At the same time, you can feel good about what you are doing because it's cleaner burning fuel made right here in Iowa. And it's just a little step in the direction of lessening dependence on foreign oil sold by people who hate America."

<hr/>

The campaign was a success—of sorts. We created a demand knowing we would lose money. There was no way to make money on the biodiesel at the time. Even selling it to the farmers at a premium, we were upside down by fifty cents per gallon. Making money wasn't even the goal yet. It was all on a small scale. We didn't talk in industry terms then. There was no biodiesel industry. Our hopes were pinned on the Iowa farmers first, and then other diesel fuel consumers, including truckers and terminals that serve them throughout Iowa and the Midwest. We were asking them to take a chance with us and see if we could make something happen.

The fact was: there would be no way to make money ever with the small-batch production quantities we were working with. We knew that. But batch-to-batch production was all anyone knew at the time. We had to create the demand for some kind of volume production that pushed the plant to maximum capacity. We would solve the problem of what that looked like when we got there. Only then would we discover the actual value potential of biodiesel. I was trying to chase a hunch and see if we could create enough users of the product to get it in the realm of profitability.

Thankfully, I had many legitimate selling points to use in the mean time. I didn't need to use one word of balderdash. Farmers are too astute for that anyway. They are shrewd business people with the same kinds of questions I could have expected from any manager during my Purina years. If I didn't have the answer to someone's question, at least they'd pointed out something else I needed to look into. It was all part of fine-tuning our efforts. Creating a consumer base for biodiesel turned out to be a slower process than expected. But we got it done.

We had answered our three big questions. We knew we could make biodiesel that worked and guaranteed industry standards. Though our cost per gallon was not favorable, we knew what it was (or at least where we were starting from). And we knew the farmers were on board. Next we had to see if we could get the suppliers on board.

<hr/>

"You're competing with us. Why would we want to partner with you to help you do that? We rule this game. Why let you in?"

Approaching the oil companies required a totally different selling strategy. We appeared to be competing. But to us, they were customers just like the farmers. The trick was getting them to see us as a partner, a vendor supplying something they needed.

These were big-league negotiators, and they may have intimidated someone else. In fact, members of the board of directors at West Central expressed serious doubts about the odds of even getting in front of the likes of Shell, British Petroleum, Exxon-Mobil, Marathon, and others.

But Purina had groomed me for this. It was my world, an environment in which I was right at home.

We had some leverage to work with. Global environmental concern had been pointing accusatory fingers at the big oil companies for decades. We had a positive public relations element to push:

"We are creating the cleaner-burning renewable fuel you need in your product line to demonstrate that you're moving in the direction of eco-friendliness."

The conversation starter was always effective. But we would invariably be reminded of the long-standing prominence of the petroleum industry giants and their experience handling their own public realtions issues.

"Well, about that," I would counter, "isn't your age-old existence part of the problem? Yes, you've been around forever and doing the same thing forever. What can the media talk about but the negatives? We are offering you something new and fresh for everyone to talk about—something besides the boring same old story of shipping foreign oil over here, refining it, and making a lot of money. This is a new home-grown product movement away from foreign dependence and toward a cleaner environment. You could be the first of your industrial peers to be seen making a real push in renewable energy. That's something to talk about! And it gives the media something to focus on besides the protesters in the oil tanker channels down in Houston. It's really quite a big deal."

Being reminded of how small we were to be waving the "big deal" banner at them was usually next: "You're just a little co-op in Iowa. Let's imagine you've sold us on your biodiesel. How do we know you can deliver it here when we need it? What if your one plant goes down, and we can't supply our customers because we're not getting any biodiesel from you?"

"We're asking you to take a chance on us," I would acknowledge. "Until you give us a chance to prove ourselves, I can't appeal to anything but trust. Trust us. We'll do our part with timely delivery."

"Well, what kinds of transportation systems do you have in place? We're used to dealing with delivery via oil tankers and rail cars. Do have any system like that?"

We didn't. And though West Central had no history of biodiesel transactions to reference for credibility, these issues were not confronted without any track record at all. We had a pristine record of dependability in other markets. And my own experience as a former Purina executive ensuring deliverables to major national accounts over many years served as a worthy measure of credibility. I could speak their language, anticipate their questions, and respond with empathy for their concerns. That was important because one issue came down to putting my professional reputation on the line: "How can we be sure of the quality of your product, which we'll be distributing under our name? We have an international brand to protect. You're a nobody company. You've got nothing to lose. What's our quality guarantee, not just that you can make it and get it to us, but that you can deliver it over and over without a single drop of substandard quality?"

"You have my word," I would respond. "We can and will produce samples to demonstrate for you the zero-variance in our product. Come visit us in Iowa. I can show you the facility ... whatever will relieve your concern. But at this moment, that is less of an assurance than I can give with my own personal promise. If we can start our relationship there, I will back it up with whatever proof you require."

Like with the famous TV detective from the 1970s, Columbo, there was always one last question: "Our tanks are committed to our current products. We don't have any capacity available. What about storage tanks?"

Here we had a tall hurdle to jump. Physical tanks were expensive and tank capacity more so.

"Commit a tank to our biodiesel," I would state.

"That's a huge commitment for us to make, designating tank space for a product while waiting to see if customers will actually buy it."

"I'm asking you to take a shot with us."

That was the key to the whole thing: getting someone to roll the dice a little and take a chance. Without more history and without leverage enough to twist anyone's arm, it really came down to that. Not all would give us a go. But some did.

⁘───◎───⁘

It was all a matter of timing. We needed the farmers on board believing in the product and confident it would be available when and where they needed it. We needed the distributors on board believing the farmers would buy it if they made it available. And we needed both to happen at the same time. Things came together because of the groundwork laid through countless meetings with farmers the previous winter.

Henry Ford must have faced something like this, starting out with a car he could barely drive around his backyard a couple of times because gasoline was so hard to come by. Getting John D. Rockefeller on the phone, he probably said, "Hey John, where are the service stations? I have a great product here, but how do I sell cars if people can't get any fuel to run them? Give me stations. We need gas!"

That's the way it was for us.

"OK, I'll buy," a farmer would say. "But deliver it to me here when I need it."

Distributors said the same thing. Getting the farmers and the oil companies on board had to converge perfectly with refining our production process and ramping up capacity, while knowing that with all of these efforts, we were still upside down in the economics.

I went to Myron and said, "If we run this old plant at absolute capacity, what do you think the cost would be … labor, methanol, machinery, everything?"

We calculated the efficiency scale—fixed costs, variable costs—and came up with a number. Then I ran it all by the West Central board of directors.

"This is fiction," they said. "These numbers are based on pure speculation."

"Yeah," I responded, "this is an all-in and see if we hit it strategy. If we can't create the volume at that price, we'll go down in flames. But if we can, I believe we'll make some money."

They said, "OK, give it a try."

I told our one salesman, Gary Haer, "That number plus ten percent is your selling price. If you sell at that price, we'll be all right. That's the target."

If you proposed a plan like this to a bunch of MBA candidates, they'd laugh you out of the classroom. But it's the way we did it, and we got our vision for running a successful biodiesel plant off the ground. It was the only chance we had.

Gary Haer ran with it, and we hit our goal. Within six months, we had the old plant at capacity—three thousand gallons a day—and we were making money. They were exciting times. Of course, the West Central board was pleased that the plant was finally converted to a money maker. And Myron, Gary, I, and others were thrilled to see our hard work paying off.

Everyone stopped calling the plant The Ol' Methyl Ester Plant and started calling it The Biodiesel Plant. We even had to shut the plant down for a few days to make the production process more efficient.

That's when the explosion happened. It left us thinking, "All that work, just to blow the thing up! "

TWENTY-SEVEN · *Stop?*

After the explosion, the big word was "Stop!"

"Stop what you're doing. It's not working!"

Actually, it had been working well. With truck drivers joining the farmers to use biodiesel, we were no longer able to keep up with demand. Nevertheless, strong reaction within our organization to a plant explosion was understandable. The entire operation was held together by management of penny-thin margins, margins we sometimes missed. Ongoing viability depended on uncertain conditions. It all still appeared a bit of a stretch. Post-explosion safety concerns added tension to the precarious balance.

My most important job on many occasions was to be a steady, calming influence. Whether in negotiations, risk management, people management, or just a strategy meeting, my aim was stability. I was successful enough that some humor developed

In times of crisis, aim for stability.

within the company related to my always maintaining the same appearance. I definitely did not always feel the same. But I did have enough confidence in the big view of our story to reassure others—usually by actions rather than words.

As time passed, some board members were content to forget about the success we'd had and just let it die. I was nearly sixty and had the sensible option of letting it go and cruising on with the success of the dairy and soybean products. But I thought: *We were just starting to see a little success. It would be a shame to let this go because of one mishap.*

While I knew the plant and our processes had nothing to do with the explosion, others were not convinced. The plant was shut down, and as we considered regrouping and taking another shot, that naturally depended on a redesigned plant. If we were going to redesign the plant, it might as well be a radical enough change to keep up with the tremendous demand increase. The time was right to get away from batch-to-batch production. Myron and I began discussing the possibilities of continuous flow.

The company's history was connected to soybeans. Soybean processing was continuous flow and very efficient. There was no waste because excess chemicals were reused. Since a continuous flow biodiesel system was nonexistent, we would have to design it. Ironically, the vision for a new and revolutionary plant was a response to a disaster—the plant explosion.

As I explained the vision to just a few people, reaction was not what I'd hoped.

"We really don't have the expertise to build a biodiesel plant."

"We don't have engineers."

"You've been successful in the ag business, but you have no construction experience. What do you know about building a refinery? And who's going to build the thing?"

The challenges were all true. Every question I faced was legitimate, and I had no answers. But just because we had no answers didn't mean we were looking at a no-go. The first step was obvious: answer the questions. If we couldn't answer the questions, we had no business continuing. It was that simple. Yes, feed and fuel are different, but they have some similarities, which we used as beginning points for connecting the dots.

I had on my team these bright country boys, Myron Danzer and Matt Schultes, who, beyond high school, had their education in common sense. I leaned on them heavily. It was time to study the industry and really learn it. They were well read and willing to dig into the project. So I fed them questions and cheered them on as they found answers. All along the way, we found elements we were familiar with and leveraged them.

Improvement can grow out of failure.

We had to find engineers who knew about liquid flow, valves, heat, and continuous systems. And we needed a builder.

West Central had a good working relationship with Todd and Sargent, a construction company that specialized in building grain elevators and feed mills across the country. They were highly reputable but knew nothing about refineries or biodiesel. I approached them with the idea of building a biodiesel plant. They were interested in the project and confident they could handle it.

Todd and Sargent was on board—a huge boost to our plans!

Agreeing with those who challenged us with questions, we created a road map to designing and building the first continuous flow biodiesel plant. It was made of answers to pertinent questions about all of the things we did not have.

TWENTY-EIGHT · *The Refinery*

The new plant would be built adjacent to the old one on the West Central Co-op complex in Ralston, Iowa, which was named for a member of the American Express Company and had no relation to the Ralston in Ralston Purina. Since we'd converted an old methyl ester plant into a biodiesel plant, we put up with many things in the first plant that we wanted to address in the new one.

Of course, the main focus and expense of the design was continuous flow. Getting away from making the biodiesel in batches would be a boon in three ways: one, it would give us optimal control over the process; two, it would redefine capacity and show us just how far we could go with biodiesel; and three, it would create greater credibility in the eyes of big oil companies and distributors. It would be a state-of-the-art refinery, much more like what they were used to dealing with.

The design began with an elaborate pretreatment process where unwanted fatty elements and contaminants would be separated and removed, leaving only what was to be used in refining the biodiesel. Then the refining process was designed based on repetitive centrifuging, washing, and filtering the oil on the molecular level to make it pure diesel.

Between the pretreatment and refinement sides of the process, every detail of the system would be monitored in a computer control room. Biodiesel samples would be tested every two hours in a fully functional laboratory on a composite shift basis, enabling us to exceed industry standards for quality control.

Another important factor we wanted to address was storage. We designed the plant with a 1.5 million gallon biodiesel storage capacity in three tanks, and crude feed stock storage in three other tanks. Here again, it meant more expense up front to build the plant, but it gave us much more control over the logistics.

Safety was emphasized in every detail of every nook and cranny of the new design. Some people might have thought we were overdoing it considering the added expense of implementing foolproof safety systems throughout the factory. But experience showed us there was no such thing as overdoing it on safety.

Lastly, the design allowed for nothing to be wasted in the entire process. Removed glycerin would be sold for use in body lotions, toothpaste, cosmetics, detergents, and other products to companies such as Proctor and Gamble. Free fatty acids would be used in animal and poultry feed as an energy ingredient. Since we were creating a cleaner-burning renewable fuel, we wanted the very process to be just as environmentally friendly.

By the time we finished designing the new plant, we knew biodiesel through and through. And we knew our continuous flow plant would be the only one of its kind.

Over the couple of years since we'd started, an actual biodiesel industry had begun taking shape. More and more, this fledgling industry looked like it had enormous potential. We were at its leading edge.

Unfortunately, potential is often a pretty tough sell. It is easier to be persuasive with hard numbers. But in our case, the firmest number we knew was on the cost side of building the new refinery: $12 million.

It was time to present all of the information to the West Central board. Typically, when presenting a proposal for a large investment, you define industry parameters and make a case for the percentage of the industry investors can expect to secure through the venture.

Normally, when dealing with established industries, even if the investment number is large, the industry percentage number is very small. Single digits or fractions are expected. This is because the industry mass justifies the investment, and a large investment securing a minute share of the industry can result in exceptional returns.

When we got to that part of my presentation to the board, the numbers were awkward if not comical. Our proposed $12 million plant would produce twelve million gallons of biodiesel annually. What percentage of the US biodiesel industry was that? Well, the total industry was only three million gallons of annual biodiesel. This meant that according to my presentation, one quarter of our production capacity assumed complete domination of the existing industry. Three quarters of our production was aimed at an industry that did not yet exist.

I was not just attempting to sell the board on the merits of the new plant. I was presenting an educated forecast of where the young industry was headed. I was selling the conviction that with the new plant, we could define the industry itself and set its course. It would have come across as lunacy if not for one thing: I believed whole-heartedly we would do exactly that.

TWENTY-NINE · *REG*

The wind in New York is ever shifting, but steady. It blows hotdog wrappers across crowded streets and back. It aids or hinders baseballs and footballs in ballparks and stadiums whimsically, seemingly according to moods. While pushing sailboats here and there along the Hudson River, it makes flags dance in front of the home of the United Nations. Wreaking havoc on newsstands, vendors try to stay connected to Yankee's caps with one hand while selling newspapers with the other.

"Nile, look at this. You're in *The New York Times*!"

Jeff Stroburg had bought a paper as we walked through Times Square. We were in New York City on a capital-raising mission. Not only did we carry the clout of "Chairman of the Board" and "President" of our company when making presentations and entering negotiations, but we were also an excellent team in the entire process of raising capital. As great teammates do, one of us always caught the detail the other might have missed.

"Sure enough, look at that," I answered, seeing a dramatic image of myself in the paper, hands stretched out and toward the viewer like some titan commissioning minions to go forth and do his bidding. The photographer had actually caught me at an unusually expressive moment while I was answering an otherwise ordinary question in front of potential investors.

> Branding is tricky; too much new at once can alienate.

In the article, the name of the company I was representing was not West Central Co-op. It was REG (Renewable Energy Group). As we had gotten more into the biodiesel project and had begun enjoying success, we knew we needed a different name. However, branding is tricky. When you are trying to create consumer demand by starting with customers from other areas of your established business, it's not a good time to change names. New product, new relationships, new name—too much new at once can alienate. So we kept West Central Co-op as a rule, but made use of REG in reference to its biodiesel division. Eventually, success accumulated sufficiently to warrant exclusive use of the name REG for the biodiesel company capable of standing on its own merits.

Accumulated success also led us to New York for the capital-raising mission. But taking a start-up division of West Central Co-op (once most notable for having blown up its only plant) to representation before investors in New York was as unlikely a path as getting from Hog-Chow to biodiesel. We did it by accumulating something else: credible partners.

THIRTY · *Partners*

The diesel engine has been around since the late nineteenth century. The diesel industry had all that time to create infrastructure. Logistically, we were more than a century behind. The push to create consumer demand meant we needed to simultaneously create a local biodiesel infrastructure of availability. Both had been successful enough to warrant the proposal to build a new plant.

When the board of directors gave us the OK to go forward with construction of the new plant, it was more of a beginning than arrival; it came with the understanding that continuing in biodiesel was a huge, expensive operation. A new $12 million refinery was just the start of it. Laying the foundations of West Central's new product division was "hook-and-worm" with advancing the biodiesel industry.

We knew we could make the product. We knew we could increase its demand. We didn't know who would help us connect those two dots. While the plant was being built, we had to continue building relationships.

The distribution strategy was simple: connect to a really good existing system. But simple was far from easy. The infant biodiesel industry needed to be assimilated into the infrastructure of the century-old diesel industry. Our approach to large petroleum companies was already one of seeing them as customers, not competitors. But we needed more diplomacy to get them to warm up to us and see us as friend, not foe. The same had to be done with big-truck service stations, like Flying J, Love's, Pilot, and Road Ranger. All this had to be done in a way that avoided conflict of interest. We were not in a position to alienate any players in the field.

We also needed to grow our staff to handle the demands of all we attempted to do. But the growth had to be slower than we preferred, not in keeping with the exponentially growing workload, but a risky pace or two ahead of the company's bottom line growth. Though the workload was ten times the capacity of our staff, we could not simply go on a hiring spree to fill the gap. Asking everyone to work ten times the hours was not the answer either. Everyone had to be challenged to work smarter, with passion and optimal efficiency.

In challenging times like those, you see the character of people come forward. Discovering how people respond to seemingly impossible workload and deadline pressures can be an adventure. We had some terrific people in place. But before we could add anyone, we got smaller. A guy quit.

It took a while, but we filled the opening by hiring a twenty-seven-year-old named Paul Nees (pronounced Nās, rhyming with race) from Minnesota. Paul was a native

Iowan and wanted to relocate in his home state. West Central

Hire passion
and persistence.

Co-op was exactly where he wanted to be and tailor-made for his abilities. I know because he told me several times over the course of the year in which we delayed hiring him. The kind of passion and persistence he used to convince me to bring him on board was precisely what we wanted on our team.

On Paul's first day, he was directed to a desk in a backroom office space. On his desk, he found an eight-and-a-half-by-eleven sheet of paper containing descriptions of what the person he was replacing had done. Everything else expected of him was in my head. I needed help developing protocols and procedures to procure soybean oil, sell glycerin by-products, and work with biodiesel-specific risk management. Because no industry was in place, we had to create everything as we went along.

Hiring Paul was a throwback to my Purina days, though downsized to an extreme. At Purina, we hired twenty bright go-getters like Paul at a time and plugged them into specific places in a fine-tuned development program.

At West Central, Paul would learn firsthand the meaning of the term "baptism by fire." Paul initially would require more of my time, but he presented an opportunity for me to mentor and delegate responsibility—in that order. And he would quickly prove to be a great asset to the company. One of West Central's first Biodiesel Division hires, Paul would have a privileged perspective, participating in a remarkable construction from the ground up. The unique position would not always be enviable.

One of the impressive things along the journey was seeing many people like Paul come together from many different directions but with the same commitment to discovering the best solutions. They were doing their part in some phase of the indispensable process of due diligence. Even when we encountered resistance, it was usually for a good reason and forced us to address things we had not yet considered. Surprise partnership opportunities arose because we were knocking on so many doors connected to many other doors.

Immediately upon opening, the new plant was a huge success. It was at capacity in no time because of diligent relationship building. In turn, the sophisticated new plant facilitated more partnerships. It was not always easy to get corporate decision-makers in San Francisco, Houston, Dallas, DC, or New York to visit the plant in Ralston, Iowa. But once they did, a new image of our little biodiesel-producing refinery was forged, and they took us much more seriously in terms of partnership.

Soon we were in growing relationships with partners across many industries: the farmers producing the soybeans to run the plant and buying the biodiesel, the construction company Todd and Sargents, petroleum terminals like HWRT, Procter and Gamble and other companies using glycerin and other processing by-products, and numerous truck lines and service station chains.

Build relationships.

150

As they say, success breeds success. It is also difficult to keep secret. With Iowa being an important stop along the campaign trail and our company being a leader in renewable fuel, politicians made our tiny, out-of-the-way spot on the map a priority destination.

We were proud of what we had done and were eager to show it off. Before we knew it, plant tours were part of the weekly schedule. But this was somewhat naïve. Others out there were trying to figure out this biodiesel thing. Indiscriminate tour invitations helped them. Belatedly realizing that fact, we quickly restricted tours of our new plant.

The next question was inevitable:

"Should we be satisfied with just one plant?"

We encountered the predictable objections to the idea of building more plants:

"You're just a small agricultural company with one success in biodiesel. Now you want to shoot off in a whole new direction and build refineries?"

Once again, all challenges had a sensible basis. Building refineries demanded huge capitalization. We were not in that position. We had our own plant built, and it was doing well. But we were cash poor after making it happen. And with other divisional operations, West Central did not have unlimited funds to invest in biodiesel.

We had been making money with the new refinery, but we knew the business could be much bigger. We just didn't have the working capital for the next step. We also wanted to stay in the lead in the biodiesel industry, which had gained the attention of many business people. The goal was to build and operate our own refineries. The challenge was getting there.

In 2005, I asked my two employee partners, Myron Danzer and Gary Haer, if they thought other investment entities would hire us to build refineries for them. We didn't know the answer. We did know that someone had to manage the refinery, someone had to procure the feedstock, and someone had to sell the finished product. And no one else was doing it at our level. So, if the idea had any shot of working, we would probably have to handle all of those roles for our clients, not just building the refineries.

The question was adjusted to: "Would someone hire us to build and manage a refinery for them? Could we make a business out of that?"

We were pleased to find out that the answer was "Yes." A few investment groups were interested in the idea—or at least interested in discussing it.

In a year or so, we were selling, building, and running refineries for others. This was all based on the model developed at West Central and all possible because of that success. This all began with the question: "Would anyone pay us to do this?" Once again, we were looking at something totally new, something that needed to be invented. There's no road map in a new industry.

Just as experience taught us what issues to address when designing the new $12 million plant, running it and discovering the real demand potential for biodiesel led to more expensive adjustments in the new breed of biodiesel plant for the new venture.

The main plant function to be addressed this time was dependence on soybean oil as the only feedstock the plant could run on. Depending on one raw material meant being chained to its market performance—a potentially precarious situation.

To better manage our margins, we had to be diversified in our feedstock usage. Our first plant locked us in to soybean oil. In the new design, soybean oil would be one of several feedstock options, such as beef tallow, poultry fat, choice white grease from the swine industry, and used cooking oil.

Each must be processed a little differently, so that would mean more initial expense in the design and building of the plant—a several million-dollar difference. But it would bring much greater efficiency and better control of our margins in the long run. It would also keep us ahead of the game in biodiesel as we built and managed the only plants capable of running on multiple sources of feedstock.

Rumor was that some of the big boys in the agriculture industry—Cargill, Louis Dreyfus, ADM—were getting into biodiesel. Their financial resources were far superior to ours. Plants run on soybean oil would be their focus because of vested interest in that commodity. Diversity in feedstock options would enable us to maintain some cost advantage.

Often ingenuity and bold decisions are rewarded by great timing. Finding out that someone else is ahead of the game with a piece of the infrastructure essential to your needs is one such welcome surprise. That was the case with the discovery of a company that gathered restaurant greases. It was at the other end of the feedstock equation, and it had devised an efficient system to remove used cooking oil from fast-food restaurants and supply them with fresh oil. Partnering with that company gave us a base feedstock option we could count on.

Success breeds success.

The next big thing to address was production capacity. We needed to increase it quite a bit. Our new plants would produce thirty million gallons of biodiesel a year. This was the most expensive of the design adjustments. And safety continued to be a big and expensive priority: $4 million of explosion-inspired safety features were included in the new plant designs.

Then there were the advanced logistical features. The plants were designed to be built along rail systems to accommodate rail distribution. They also had four bays for eighteen-wheelers: two to receive feedstock supplies and two for filling tankers with biodiesel to deliver throughout the country. The price tag of the new plants was $40 million.

Our business model evolved into a two-contract process. One contract was for the refinery. The other was for the management services, which turned out to be the far more complex of the two. Every management contract entailed hiring purchasing professionals, chemical engineers, and sales and marketing staff; operating the plant; leasing rail cars and arranging other transportation; and making contacts throughout the United States or abroad so every refinery had access to the best biodiesel markets.

Spending $40 million on a refinery was not easy for an investment group to get their collective minds around. The selling process took awhile—twenty meetings or so. As they weighed the idea against other investment opportunities, we had to sell them on why this was the best and why we were the ones to do it. The investors who bought plants from us were new to biodiesel. So we spent hours and hours teaching them.

Because we did not have money, we looked to the new plan of building plants for other businesses. Ironically, because of building plants for customers with more money, we were able to really go for it with our plant design and fully develop our "ideal" plant. Again, the industry moved forward as a result.

The first multiple feedstock plant was built for investors in Albert Lea, Minnesota. The second was built in Andy William's hometown, Wall Lake, Iowa. The next was in Newton, Iowa. Across the street from the plant in Newton is another renewable energy company, a windmill manufacturer. Those few acres of real estate are like a portrait of the changing face of industry.

The town of Newton, Iowa, was originally built around the appliance manufacturer, Maytag. Once the biggest and best of all appliance companies, distributing all over the world, Maytag lost the margins battle and was bought out by RCA, who subsequently moved the company elsewhere. That left a huge hole in the Newton economic base.

The hole turned out to be fortunate for REG. It was probably the main reason Newton investors were willing to take a shot on a $40 million biodiesel refinery. In turn, owners of the Newton refinery benefited from the glut of skilled technicians left behind when RCA pulled the plug on Newton's Maytag plant.

We needed the benefit of such fortuitous situations and whatever other help we could get. My Purina management experience came in handy as well. You don't always know everything you'd like to know. And if you—the leader—don't know, there is no way those you are leading can know.

REG was in uncharted territory. We had to hire skill set qualities and put them in place where needed at the moment of hire, but knowing they were professionals with much greater capabilities than we were initially putting to use. You might call it projection hiring—hiring a person who was willing to perform a role at the current production, sales, and distribution capacity but capable of handling radically enlarged demand. I would say, "Look, what you see before you today is not what this is ultimately going to look like. I can tell you the vision, but I can't show it to you presently." And high-level professionals took those positions on that basis.

Hire good character and skilled people who will get the work done.

Throughout the process of hiring, I explained what I knew, what the plan was, what needed to be done, and that there was risk ... we might fail or succeed. But if they accepted a job offer, I insisted they work with passion, treating the company and its future as if it were their own.

It comes down to intelligent flexibility and dexterity, identifying what needs to be done and putting high character, skilled people to work getting it done. Sometimes the roles are defined through that process. In the case of REG, people hired in that situation are still at the company in executive roles.

◦ ◦ ◦ ◦ ◦ ▱▱▱▱▱◉▱▱▱▱▱ ◦ ◦ ◦ ◦ ◦

Before long, we had numerous plants in operation, producing and distributing millions of gallons of biodiesel annually. We had hundreds of individual contracts with third-party businesses purchasing the biodiesel from the various plants. We managed all of it—production, procurement, sales, and supply chain. And everything was working as it should, which was remarkable since legally they were complex arrangements.

We started the business of selling and managing refineries to build capital and to keep the momentum of success going. Eventually, there came a time of now-or-never to push for the initial goal of building and running our own refineries. We needed a $100 million capital-raising campaign.

What began as dialog with Iowa farmers to see if we could create demand for biodiesel had become greater demand than anyone could have imagined. The dialog narrowed to just the farmers who made up the West Central board of directors. When the REG vision eclipsed West Central's commitment to the biodiesel side of the business, the new REG board of directors took over the dialog from there.

Members of that board were a mix of farmers from West Central, lawyers, and executive businessmen like me. Having been raised on a farm, I am proud to say the farmers hardly stood out in that environment. They were business-savvy, margin-conscious and astute, as shrewd as an arrow is straight, generally hitting the bulls-eye with insightful questions directed at their peers around the table. And while REG was no longer a division of West Central Co-op, West Central continued to be a critical partner as a financial investor in the business.

The investors I approached next were similarly part of a vital and ongoing relational thread. But in this case, it reached back to my Purina days. When steering Purina through the transition to independence from Ralston, my research project with those cattle ranchers in Texas and New Mexico pointed us to a new strategy: offering our customers firm forward pricing on feed supplies. But we couldn't do that on our own. Offering firm forward pricing to our customers was dependent upon suppliers committing to do the same for us. And two major suppliers had stepped up and made that commitment: Bunge and ED&F Man.

Because we shared a long relational history and because they were willing to hear me out about one revolutionary project, I called on my friends at Bunge and ED&F Man to see what their interests in biodiesel might be. Once again, I had a need, a need for financial backing. And, I was coming from a position of far less relational leverage than that of an officer of Purina. But once again, they were willing to hear me.

Preparing for the meetings was all about telling the story well. There was one chance to inspire further consideration and more dialog. Those at the presentations were lawyers and number-crunching executives looking out for their company's best interest. And of course, approaching industry leaders who have the resources to take a good idea and run with it themselves, I had a few practical questions:

Relationships matter.

If I convince them of the industry potential in front of us, why would they direct their financial resources my way? Why not just commit to starting biodiesel divisions in their companies and build their own refineries? Why not seize the opportunity for themselves? Why even mess with me or a little-known company like REG?

But ego-in-equilibrium is part of all business environments. The only way a company representative would raise a hand and recommend running with the idea themselves was if he or she could do as good a job as me in answering questions about how it would get done.

Among top professionals, credibility is always on the line. Yes, they probably could do it themselves. But would they? No large company has an idle component waiting for something to do. Everything is running at maximum efficiency. So taking on something new is a big deal.

And one factor stood out above all else: I had the passion! I was already invested in the project and had a vision that was many layers into established infrastructure. I knew the story intimately from the beginning, having been involved in its development.

Just as important, I could tell it in their language—the layered economics of soybean crushing or commodity logistics—because I knew that industry. I wielded belief that was backed by proven commitment to doing the work.

As it turned out, both companies had biodiesel on their radar before I called them. They were interested. Over the course of many more meetings, interest was fashioned into financial partnership.

With the capital commitment of West Central, Bunge, and ED&F Man, it was time to pursue new relationships. All signs pointed to New York. That's how I came to be standing near the newsstand in Times Square with Jeff Stroburg, looking at the newspaper bearing my image.

It was somewhat surreal. We were in New York because we had amassed enough success to take a shot at the bigger vision for REG, but we still had to get bigger money behind us. We were there to meet with Goldman Sachs, Morgan Stanley, UBS, Credit Suisse, and other prominent capital-funding organizations.

While the meetings themselves were similar to those with the partners already on board, the process was different. The large capital investment companies each have a multitude of investment funds. Gaining financial investors through them was based on a stair-step model.

First we met with the actual companies (UBS, for example). They wanted to know if our story was credible. If they liked it, they looked over their portfolio of investors and advertised REG's plan to those who might be a good fit (such as investors interested in emerging renewable energies or fuel technologies). We were put in touch with those interested and met with them.

Everyone Jeff Stroburg and I met during this process was highly educated, with multiple post-graduate degrees—usually an MBA and a law degree. Even though we knew our story so well, their questions challenged us. And behind them were teams of people checking everything out. No stone was unturned. If we could answer all of their questions satisfactorily, we would win their confidence. Winning their confidence meant they believed in REG and that it could make money.

Many of the investment groups liked our idea but did not want to invest in REG. Others were interested based on the initial presentation. But that only meant we began a type of courtship with numerous meetings. The interested parties progressively narrowed to a small field of investors who were serious about a financial commitment to REG. These investors visited Ralston or Newton, Iowa, to tour refineries.

The process from the original meetings with the large New York companies to potential investors arriving at a plant for a tour took about six months. All the due diligence was about laying cash on the line. This is the capital market place. This is how it works if you have a good idea. We had to find investors who would put their confidence in us. We could not have gone forward without them.

When I look back, I'm amazed to think we were able to find anyone to believe in REG enough to entrust large sums of money to us. Yes, investors would receive shares of REG. But the company was not public yet, so they were not tradable shares. The money was not loans to be paid back. This was capital investment with no strings attached ... with zero guarantees.

Something else still amazes me. As Jeff and I met with investors, their main question was this: "Do you know anything about managing risk?"

REG was a biodiesel producer. We were instrumental in launching the biodiesel industry. We had built and managed numerous refineries that accounted for most of the industry volume. Yet, not one investor led with a question about biodiesel technologies. Yes, they wanted us to give an account of our technological knowledge and financial numbers supporting it, but not until after answering questions about risk management performance.

"Commodities are 75 percent of the cost structure," they would say. "We want to know what kind of command you have of managing commodities risk to protect our investment."

When I left college and looked for a job, commodity trading was not on my radar. I became familiar with the practice on the job. It was the skill I enjoyed most from my very first position as a manager trainee at Ralston Purina. It was at the heart of the merchandising specialization encouraged by executives who guided my early career. It was the basis for redesigning the Purina business model to thrive independently of Ralston. It was number one among the listed requirements on West Central's search for someone to manage their dairy, soybeans, and feed divisions—the job that rescued me from middle-aged unemployment. Once again, in pursuing investment partners, risk management was critical to moving forward.

Credibility is always on the line.

I was able to answer the question with unwavering confi-

156

dence, able to assure proficiency in the area of primary concern. Consequently, we completed our financial partners with the additions of NGP Energy Technology Partners and Natural Gas Partners. We had our $100 million.

THIRTY-ONE · *The Bell*

Early in his career, Ronald Reagan worked at the radio station WHO. With its fifty-thousand-watt signal, it reaches listeners from coast to coast. But Des Moines, Iowa, is its home, and the Midwest heartland is its target audience.

As REG became known throughout Iowa, people became more interested in biodiesel. One day in 2007—right after REG was named Iowa Company of the Year—I received a call from someone at WHO asking me to join a couple of the station's radio hosts to talk about REG. The show received excellent response, and I became "Mr. Biodiesel."

Mr. Biodiesel became a semi-regular radio phenomenon—perhaps not quite a sensation. I joked that Mr. Biodiesel was an on-air hit because he had a face for radio. The same show hosts would have me on now and then to report on REG and update the public on the biodiesel industry. Over the course of a couple of years, I did about forty radio spots. While I had many opportunities to plug our company, I also enjoyed the chance to educate listeners. I was often able to take their calls and answer questions directly.

This indicated the growing interest in biodiesel and the ascending success of REG, an ascent noticed well beyond Iowa borders. Around the same time that we made the pages of *The New York Times,* we were written up in the *Houston Chronicle.* In 2008, *Inc.* magazine named REG number seven on its list of fastest growing companies in the energy sector, and number thirty-one among companies from all categories intending to go public.

Business 2.0 followed by naming REG as one of its "disruptors" who would change the way people had done business for years and stated, "REG is one of the fifteen companies that will change the world."

Who would've thought all this hubbub could start with one little invitation back at West Central: "We have this plant … methyl ester production. Why don't you see what you can do with that?"

But once we started, the momentum continued. Aside from the acclaim from prominent publications and the fun of radio spots, there was a video featuring President George W. Bush, Willie Nelson, Neil Young, and yours truly, "Mr. Biodiesel."

The video showed Neil Young filling the tank of his RV with biodiesel, saying, "It's the most patriotic thing I've ever done." He also stated, "Everything about the world today points to this as a solution."

Celebrate your successes.

Neil predicted that people would begin using biodiesel "to demonstrate they don't want foreign oil. They'll do it to support the American farmer, and they'll do it just because it makes them feel good environmentally."

President Bush made similar statements: "For the sake of energy security, for the sake of economic security, we need more ethanol and biodiesel. ... I envision a time when someone will come to me and say, 'Well, Mr. President, the corn crop is up, we're growing more soybeans in America, and we're less dependent on foreign sources of oil as a result of it.'"

One image showed a decal on the back of Willie Nelson's brand new Mercedes that read, Powered by Biodiesel. Willie cited biodiesel as "the light at the end of the tunnel ... our way to grow our way out of the situation we find ourselves in."

The video also showed a US Navy ribbon-cutting ceremony, commemorating the Navy's breakthrough commitment to biodiesel use. When asked about the future of biodiesel use in the Navy—the largest user of diesel fuel in the world—Captain Paul Grossgold declared it "almost unlimited," due to the fact that " we can use it anywhere we can use petro-diesel right now."

One of my own contributing statements was a forecast: "We think the demand can grow to a billion gallons as soon as we can build plants."

A billion! Just a few years earlier I had presented the West Central board of directors with a plan to build a new plant that included the audacious projection of twelve million gallons of annual production—four times the industry output at the time.

In late 2013, the NFL contracted REG to supply the fuel to run its entire two-week production of the 2014 Super Bowl. Around that same time, it was announced that the biodiesel industry had eclipsed the billion-gallon mark for 2013. Just a couple of months later, REG published its 2013 financials. Sales were $1.5 billion, and earnings were $186 million.

When my thirty-three-year Purina career ended on a sour note in the late 1990s, Purina's earnings were around $170 million. The last thing on my mind at the time was the possibility of starting a company whose performance would surpass that of Purina in just ten years. Those were difficult days. My ultimate firing after the company was bought by Koch Industries was on the heels of a second failed attempt to become Purina's CEO. And I faced numerous rejections while trying to land on my feet, hoping some company would value my professional experience. I had job offers. But they generally required starting over professionally. My one good offer had come from the small Iowa company called West Central Cooperative.

The series of events was humbling. But humble is the word I would use to characterize my career. I was as surprised as anyone by successes along the way. And every success happened because of various things coming together just right, none of which were under my control, and none of them part of any master plan I laid out.

In fact, in most cases, I would have done things differently if I'd been able to. Topping that list would be the default landing at West Central. Not in my wildest imagination could I have anticipated that job turning into the opportunity of a lifetime.

I returned to New York in 2012, not to raise money, but to celebrate. REG had successfully gone public. I was there to help "ring the bell" at NASDAQ. I was there to get my smiling face on the colorful, electronic, eight-story NASDAQ billboard above Times Square. It wasn't on my bucket list. I had never aimed for this. But after all that hard work, it sure was fun. It was an exciting time.

I was there for the whole ride. We'd started in the back room of an office space, a side business of a farmer's co-op located in Ralston, Iowa. From there, we not only launched a company doing business with all the big boys of the industry, but also played the lead role in launching the biodiesel industry. Even as demand swelled and more major players came into our market, we maintained our position as industry leader. Only a handful of opportunities like that exist in any generation.

THIRTY-TWO · *The Unseen*

Spirit wind is the most mysterious of all. It is the defining source of a "commodity" of great worth but often least valued: faith. Discussing the difference between physical and spiritual matters with a man named Nicodemus, Jesus said, "The wind blows where it wishes, and you hear its sound, but you do not know where it comes from or where it goes. So it is with everyone who is born of the Spirit."

My Christian faith has provided a solid footing throughout my life. That is not a statement on how I have lived it sure-footedly, but rather of how well it has served me even when my own dexterity has been sorely lacking along this grand journey.

Much like the unseen but unmistakable guidance of executives in St. Louis moving my early career along, my journey has benefited from providential foresight and appointment. When I look back, even in adverse circumstances—maybe especially then—I see God's fingerprints.

Listen for the Spirit.

There was a time when English tradition made it seem like being a firstborn would have made my life better. But being the second born in our family developed my determination to overcome obstacles.

Similarly, it appeared that I might have benefited from having a larger measure of the mechanical abilities and interests my brother and dad had. But not being a part of their bonding time forced me to recognize my true interests and abilities. As a result, a more solitary path shaped my character. Countless hours training and being trained by horses ingrained in me the importance of trust in relationships and patience in problem solving.

After shoveling who knows how many tons of hog manure over the course of my youth, I planned to leave agriculture behind for a business career. Instead, my business career ensured that I was never far from farms and their products (and scents). Thankfully, someone looking out for me from above knew me better than I did and ignored those "farewell to agriculture" aspirations!

My career benefited from instincts fashioned in the corn and soybean fields of my Iowa upbringing. I had firsthand appreciation of sunup-to-sundown labor and a place of responsibility in the hierarchical structure of community.

Some people like the idea of farming and the American farmer. I knew the reality. And while I did move from the family farm, farming habits never got out of me. Even after my career supplied plenty of means to hire landscaping and lawn care services, I came home and handled the homestead labor myself. Working land felt like closeness to God. It was in my soul.

While stationed in Bloomington, Illinois, I felt deeply convicted about the estrangement from my father that had continued for more than a decade. For years, I had felt like it was his fault and his responsibility to care enough about me, his son, to initiate reconciliation.

Finally, I decided enough was enough. After arranging a trip to Iowa, I dedicated my time there to helping him around the farm and just hanging out with him. I would have liked the subject to come up, to officially put the relationship break behind us. But we didn't say a word about it—ever.

Yet, even without that, we had four wonderful years—the most intimate father-son years of my entire life—of many hours enjoying one another's company before he passed in 1978.

Don't wait to forgive.

Though he knew he had a heart condition, Dad had no ability to downshift a little in his later years. He died of a sudden heart attack at age sixty-three. I thank God I did not wait one minute longer to act on the forgiveness I had in my heart all along.

Some time later, I was talking with a colleague at Ralston Purina, Bob Reeves, whose sales region had included Iowa. Bob told me about a time when he had gone to our family farm to talk to my dad about some new Purina products.

"Do you know my son, Nile Ramsbottom?" Dad had asked.

Bob responded, "No, but I've heard the name."

"Well, keep an eye out for him," Dad said. "One day, he's going to be really something in that company."

Hearing those words was an emotional experience. Even now, their recollection moves me. I remember thinking about all those years we'd been estranged while he had those thoughts and feelings about me—thoughts and feelings I didn't have the privilege to know about. Even so, the healing power they gave me was amazing. I am grateful for little graces like a conversation with a friend who knew my dad back-when.

There is a well-known expression, "We don't have a prayer." Well, that describes the way things looked to me as I headed for the microphone to make that presentation before top managers in New Orleans, Louisiana. There I was, the king of preparation. Obviously I would have preferred being prepared and having a team of genuine helpers. Or perhaps, I would have preferred just not being in that situation. But being there and being at a loss helped me recognize the ensuing success was not my own, but relational. God's favor was near and evident in that moment.

Consequently, I knew the following promotion to vice president of Purina's western region was by more than an earthly appointment. That was comforting to know as I took responsibility for managing 1,400 employees.

And the best example of guiding help was the job at West Central Cooperative. Not only did I "not have a prayer." I could not have imagined praying for the things that conspired to take me there. I thought being forced out of Purina was a catastrophic turn of events. Finding employers uninterested in my over-qualified services after months of job hunting felt like an insult.

But those experiences resulted in my being exactly where I needed to be to hear the Holy Spirit so clearly tell me to keep going in my focus to find a job. That was the part I treasure most.

While I have never been demonstrative or outspoken regarding my faith, it has been a constant of encouragement and meaning, nonetheless.

THIRTY-THREE · *A Sudden Blackness*

One of the scariest things my faith saw me through showed up in a startling way in 2004. It made a lasting impression about human frailty—my own!

Thanks to my upbringing on the farm, disciplines of physical activity were woven into my personal constitution and never left me. Neither did my love for horses. I continued to ride and train horses throughout my adult years. This hobby required me to be in at least decent shape. And I pursued the hobby in addition to fifty-hour workweeks mostly spent on my feet, yard work during evenings and weekends, and an active relationship with Terry that never seemed to leave the dating phase. I didn't leave room for sedentary ways to creep in.

But in terms of real physical fitness, another hobby kept me slim and trim. I had taken up tennis as an adult and participated in competitive league play. The US Tennis Association was an organized environment in which I was able to grow as a singles player, eventually winning the Midwest regional championship in the fifty and older division.

I took for granted my ability to feel great, move around nimbly, and add whatever activities could be fit into a day.

Then one tiny yet enormous issue abruptly halted my days of taking good health for granted.

While Terry and I were visiting friends in Omaha, I got up one morning and had a black curtain in my field of vision. I quickly discovered that the problem was in my left eye. Blackness. All I did was get up out of bed. There it was.

We drove somewhere, and the problem persisted. I called a doctor. He said, "It sounds like you have a detached retina."

He did a few tests and told me I needed surgery immediately: that day.

The surgery went well, and the eye healed with no residual effects to my vision. What a relief!

But six months later, the same thing happened again: sudden blackness, like a curtain in my field of vision. This time, however, the emergency surgery was performed on my right eye. During the following year, it happened two more times. Two more surgeries were performed on my right eye.

Be open to grace.

I was mad at the doctors for not being able to fix the problem.

I was mad at God for allowing the miserable intrusion to my important plans and activities. We were in the middle of surging REG momentum. I had a million things to do. Needing one eye surgery was bad enough, but multiple surgeries caused me to feel insecure about where this was headed ... insecurity about when I would next open my eyes and see blackness.

During a lifetime of taking good health for granted, it had never occurred to me to say, "Hey, what's up with that?"

But when something impaired my vision and compromised mobility and my way of life, I was upset and asking questions. Physical fragility had exposed another kind of frailty.

One day, as I wrestled with the anger and the questions, I suddenly felt an unexplainable peace. I saw something more clearly than ever before: grace. There it was, just as unexpected as the blackness. Grace ... tender, undeserved, and purging all the insecurity.

<hr/>

You try to be brave. You pray.

No one ever thinks they'll be told they have cancer. The word cancer is its own kind of blackness. And regardless of the symptoms preceding it, the force of its personal attachment is a thunderous kind of sudden.

Mine was prostate cancer. When I first heard the word, a million things went through my mind. But there were two main ones:

How serious is my condition?

How will this change my life?

Answer to number one: It was serious. And change? The first and immediate life change was preparing for surgery. The series of eye surgeries seemed far behind me, though they had happened only a few years earlier. And they were not what I consider as "major" surgery.

This was.

I had faith that God was with me and was resolved to embrace His will in whatever the outcome. If the cancer could not be cured, I was willing to live, for however long, dealing with that reality in the confidence of His care. But that is not to say I was without trepidation.

Being lifted from the gurney and moved to the operating table was an ominous moment. *This is really going to happen.*

The environment appeared chaotic with busyness and extremely orderly at the same time. Everyone was scurrying around to take care of various responsibilities. It was almost like being inside a sophisticated machine.

"You're in good hands."

"We'll take good care of you."

Soothing words from several voices was all it took. All the tensions and emotion of holding it together released, and I started to cry. I knew I was in good hands. But I was used to being in charge, taking the lead, handing out instructions. Not this time. I was trusting my life to others.

Trust others.

Coming out of surgery felt strangely uneventful ... comfortable. Of course, anesthesia was partly responsible for that. But

168

I had indeed been well taken care of. The surgery was a success. More importantly, several years of cancer-free reports have followed the surgery. Perhaps the biggest life change has been the lasting impression: mortal!

THIRTY-FOUR · *Mentoring*

One of the most rewarding aspects of a half-century career has been a direct outworking of deeply held beliefs: mentoring. Discipleship is intrinsic to Christian thought and intention. The more popular word in current use is mentoring.

Whichever word you use, the concept is rooted in an obligation to pass along virtue and its empowerment to the next generation. It all circles back to relationship.

We are not islands. We are not here to soak up the sun, feel the tide's lovely caress along our personal, well-kept boundaries, and be the focal point of beautiful scenery.

We are here for each other and, in my view, for God's pleasure. And what else would our Creator take greater pleasure in than seeing His children care for one another well.

I am gratified to know that people I mentored at Purina are still there in upper management positions, and those mentored at REG are intrinsic to its ongoing success and that of its burgeoning industry. They enjoy successful careers and are able to care for themselves and their families. Their excellence in work and character have led to good salaries that enable them to give back to society, not merely subsisting, but being charitable, giving generously, blessing many people.

Others have moved on to different employers, where they thrive and improve those professional environments. Foundational skills work wherever applied. Relational character is relevant across the full spectrum of human relationships.

I recall a phone call from one of my young managers, Sheila Oliver, informing me that she had fallen in love with a man in the town of her previous training. His name was David, and they had just become engaged. The town was in Missouri, and we had transferred her to Georgia.

She loved her job and could not bear the thought of jeopardizing her career with Purina, but wanted to know if she could transfer back to Missouri. Knowing we were investing a lot of money in her training in Georgia, she asked that the transfer back to Missouri take place in a year, giving enough time for the company to benefit from her current placement. I worked a few things out and was able to call her a year later to tell her of the transfer back to Missouri.

This transfer was not convenient; it was not part of our plan. But it was workable. And it was worth the unusual consideration because Sheila was more than just a valuable member of our team—she was a person with a life situation that mattered.

Build relationships by mentoring others.

Sheila rewarded Purina with years of great service. And I can't help but smile when I think of her and David being together all these years later and Sheila now enjoying a great career with John Deere in wholesale account management.

Kelly Patterson was another employee I mentored at Purina. The executive assistant who did some accounting work and kept my world organized, Kelly was not overly confident when she came to Purina. She was bashful. A series of encounters with aggressive, erratic supervisors did not help matters. It was amazing to watch her transform with just a little consideration and patient coaching. Now in Florida, Kelly is the regional operations office manager for a national commercial real estate company. People working today for Kelly—the office manager—might find it hard to believe she was once extremely shy.

Paul Nees is an accomplished young professional who's had an important role at REG from its beginning. I had the good fortune of hiring him, and I have great respect for him. Knowing that he looks to me as a mentor and a professional role model is a great honor.

And of course, there's Myron Danzer. The former high school-educated plant operations specialist is now general manager over four REG biodiesel plants. In 2013, Myron was named Iowa's Inventor of the Year by the Iowa Intellectual Property Law Association. He has two patents and one pending for his biodiesel production and purification inventions. A bit of "You'll figure it out, Myron" was all I needed to contribute. His professional position and wage are well-earned results of a strong work ethic and a hearty brand of coachability.

On many levels, I have also enjoyed coaching and teaching my sons, Greg, Mike, and Matt. Those efforts have blessed me tremendously. Things like scouting and sports can often mimic life conditions. So those were good places to ingrain principles that apply throughout all areas of life. Whether it was being the Cub Scout leader or coaching the boys in horsemanship, baseball, basketball, tennis, or fishing, things we enjoyed together were also opportunities for instruction.

Greg was a natural leader, though not the rah-rah type. In whatever sport he played, he became a team captain who led by example. A very good athlete, his determination stood out. He once rehabbed his own knee after an ACL tear by filling a five-gallon bucket with weights, sitting on the top of our washing machine, grabbing the bucket handle with his toes, and doing leg lifts.

At the time of the injury, doctors had expressed concern that Greg's sports days were over. But after his rehab program, Greg went on to play baseball all through college. He has applied the same drive in his career with Land-O-Lakes Purina trading commodities.

Mike was also a good athlete. But he was more of a fast outfielder type who loved to run. Beginning life with a heart defect, overcoming a serious physical issue was fundamental to his identity. Open-heart surgery at seven years old helped him get to his mid-twenties when his heart was fully matured and could handle a valve replacement. Meanwhile, doctors said he could play sports as long as I was the coach and watched his exertion level. In baseball, for example, that meant leaving other parents baffled when I stopped him at second or third as he ran the bases on what could have been a home run.

One impact of growing up with a heart condition was that Mike was mature for his age. Mortality consciousness and living with the anticipation of major surgery contributed to his being an unusually serious and thoughtful young man. Another impact was his choice of interest in college: chemistry and biology. All led to a career in biogenetic research focused on multiple sclerosis at Washington University in St. Louis.

Matt was the tennis player of the three. Skilled at a young age, he was also a fierce competitor. At eleven years old, he played in a regional tournament at Cherry Hills Tennis Club. Matt was far into the tournament when he encountered an opponent who was two years older and a well-known upcoming talent.

Matt appeared overmatched. But after the two battled for a couple of hours, the match came down to a diving volley at the net. When Matt got up from the hard court, his elbows and knees were bloodied, but his face told the story. He had put away the match-winning shot without regard for pain.

Years later, Matt took that same go-for-it attitude and forged a career in construction, in home remodeling.

Teaching someone how to field a grounder, return a serve, tie a hook to a fishing line, or balance a budget may seem ordinary and inconsequential. But coaching moments carry two profound messages: "You are important to me," and "How you do things matters."

There really is no reward comparable to the benefits of personal investment in others' lives.

THIRTY-FIVE · *Retirement?*

Terry and I once taught a Sunday school class to third, fourth, and fifth graders. The first week of the new class was always about meeting incoming third graders and getting a feel for the new class dynamics. On one occasion, a youngster named Bud joined us. Bud was mischievous. He was a big kid for his age and enjoyed picking on the others—nothing vicious, just annoying. More annoying to me, he was disruptive.

I was on a mission. I wanted to get something done with each class, teach something, get something beneficial across to the kids. Bud made that difficult. So when that first class was over and everyone left, I watched Bud walk away and thought, *I hope he doesn't come back next week.*

No sooner had the thought occurred when I received a clear rebuke from the Lord: "Nile, what do you think I have you here for! Bud is important to me and needs a little guidance."

I needed no second talking to. I could not have been more pleased to see Bud enter the class the next Sunday. And from then on, I did my best to be prepared every week with patience and acceptance of this little guy named Bud. In fact, I wanted to convey something of value for his sake especially. Though I never corrected him, over the course of that year, Bud's meddling behavior did change. But I never seemed to be able to get him to be attentive in class. Whether he busied himself with other activities, such as drawing or making things with paper, or whether he slouched and looked like he was sleeping, he always appeared to have his mind elsewhere.

One Sunday near the end of class as I summarized the biblical story of Naomi and Ruth, I mistakenly mixed up their names. Bud immediately corrected me: "You mean Ruth, right?"

I stopped and thought about what I'd said. He was right. He had been listening all along. In fact, no one but Bud caught the mistake.

When new third graders joined us the first week of the next year, several meddlers were among them. Partway through the first class, Bud spoke up: "Uh, look here guys … that's not the way we behave in this class. We're here to learn."

Never has a boy endeared himself to me in such a mysterious way. I was proud of him. We developed a friendship, and as we've kept in touch over the years, I have enjoyed watching him grow to be a fine young man.

Prepare with patience and acceptance.

I was Bud's Sunday school teacher for two years. But I was also the student who got the most out of that class. Bud taught me how important it is to not judge by appearance. The lesson would have a lasting impact.

For our retirement years, Terry and I had our eyes on an eastern Missouri lake community called Innsbrook. So in 2006, we built a house on lakefront property we had purchased there. But the house sat empty as the many activities leading to REG going public required more time than expected. Not until 2009, when I resigned as president and COO of REG, were we finally able to move to our new home in Innsbrook.

Even then, they were not yet retirement years. Though resigned, I maintained status as an REG employee—that of advisor to the new president and the chairman. Because I have always enjoyed sales and wanted to continue to contribute to the company in something I did well and could accomplish remotely, I also continued to serve in a sales capacity.

For some, stepping down into a lesser status after being the head of the company might be difficult. But for me, disconnecting when I knew the company could still benefit from my abilities and knowledge was what was difficult. REG was in excellent hands and no longer needed me to run it. But it was not yet a decade old and faced a growing field of formidable competition. Industry giants like Cargill, ADM, and Louis Dreyfus increasingly invested in biodiesel divisions, and other entities were trying to be the next REG. I wanted to do whatever I could to keep REG as number one in the biodiesel industry and to expand its market share where possible.

I didn't officially retire until 2013—yet here again, sort of retired. I still work for the company as a consultant. In this role, some of my most rewarding projects have been creating and teaching courses that pass on to others what I have learned over the years. Our goal is to have all key employees who will grow REG into the future—currently over four hundred—complete my three courses: "Risk Management," "The Art of Negotiation," and "Customers For Life."

The retirement side of the work is that I get to do much of the preparation side of it from our home in Innsbrook, Missouri. But teaching the courses and attending important meetings still requires me to travel to Iowa occasionally.

Before moving to Innsbrook, Terry and I wanted to be involved in the community around our home in Jefferson, Iowa. We had been blessed in many ways and wanted to pass blessings on to others. Primarily though not exclusively through our local church community, we learned of people who needed assistance that we could give. These were people who, through no fault of their own, lost jobs or faced disabilities or other circumstances that resulted in destitute conditions. We knew we could help. And as we did, we saw more opportunities to help.

One of the things Terry and I mutually cared about was helping people find employment. There is dignity in a well-earned paycheck. Many of the uncomfortable feelings related to my post-Purina unemployment situation remained fresh in our minds. It was not hard to recall days of feeling perplexed about how I had ended up out of work and why I was not finding a job. But approaching those times as though employed—keeping a schedule, being methodical about research, making phone calls, networking, filling out applications, and doing other daily job hunting tasks—taught us a lot we did not know previously about the process. It was valuable knowledge we could share with others.

It's too easy to look at others and make judgments that have no footing in reality. Sure, some people are out of work because they do not want to work. They are the exception. Many more were blindsided by adversity and are trying desperately to recover.

I only have to recall my own release from Purina or the out-of-nowhere and out-of-my-control eye problems to appreciate how a person can face devastating circumstances through no fault of his or her own.

Many people in those situations will do whatever they can to be reestablished as productive contributors to society. A helping hand is all that's needed.

Terry and I became passionate about being there for these people. After we moved to Innsbrook in 2009, the passion took on a bigger scope.

<hr />

While I was growing up, we had a big family, which meant I had a lot of aunts and uncles, and I held them all in high regard. But I always reserved a special kind of respect for my Uncle Ward. Uncle Ward was my mother's brother, and through his long career as a gunnery officer in the Army, he served in parts of three wars: World War II, The Korean War, and the Vietnam War. That can only be said of a handful of Americans.

My awe for Uncle Ward did not fade after the impressionable years of my youth. Rather, my respect for my uncle seemed to spread to all other military service men and women. I never lost sight that these people sacrificed their rights to many things the rest of us enjoyed—time with family, safety, comforts of home—to preserve their fellow Americans' rights to those very things. In many cases, their service also defended or advanced the rights of people in other countries.

So when Terry and I decided to dedicate ourselves to a ministry after settling in at Innsbrook, it was easy to determine its focus. We wanted to serve veterans.

We did not originally intend to start an organization. In the beginning, we were just interviewing existing nonprofits to find a good fit where our services were most needed. But that process ultimately revealed to us where are our hearts were drawn.

Of course, our interest in ministry was greatly driven by our faith. And the conviction about dignity in employment was also a primary motivator. These three—Christian faith, veterans, employment—were the initial thrust behind our decision to start a not-for-profit organization. Officially becoming a 501(c)(3) charitable organization in 2010, God Cares (god-cares-ministry.org) was established to minister to veterans who need help finding work and who need practical help in the process.

The faith component is behind our charitable commitment but is not something we require in those we help. The veteran emphasis is strong, ensuring that veterans have first priority in our efforts. However, we do occasionally serve non-veterans. Helping others find employment is mission critical. God Cares does not exist to support the lives of people not willing to help themselves. There are other organizations for that. God Cares exists to help others help themselves.

The scope of our service is not broad. On average, we humbly serve in three situations per week. Of course, we would like to help as many people as possible, but our vision for God Cares is not about becoming bigger and reaching further.

We take a holistic approach with each individual. The people and families served on a weekly basis—however many—are extremely important. So our vision is to become better and better at the service we provide. God Cares is entirely run by volunteers, which means all funds go directly to ministering to someone in need. We are committed to being excellent stewards of every dollar we invest in someone's life.

Making sure those we serve have the best shot at being employed often dictates the first steps in the care we give. Sound transportation, for example, is an obvious need for someone going to interviews or answering questions on an application about ability to get to work. Personal presentation impacts impression. So our ministry often includes encouragement that fosters a sense of confidence, help with proper nutrition, provision of clothing, and assistance with housing expenses to those who come to us in need.

We work closely with the Missouri Career Centers; all preparations lead to a coordinated approach to securing employment. We don't want a temporary fix. We want to provide assistance that becomes momentum toward stability and establishment in society, independent of assistance.

The undisputed MVP of God Cares is Terry. The compassion side of the ministry comes naturally to her. She knows what it is to hold things together with less than adequate means, what it is to raise a family in unstable circumstances. And the administrative side is equally her forte. I have always been one to come up with ideas. And every idea I come up with has the benefit of her administrative expertise from the beginning. God Cares is a prime example. Without Terry's diligence, insight, and capacity to manage details, it would not exist.

Helping others is the greatest reward.

We feel privileged to be involved in service to others. The name of the organization comes from personal experience. We know God cares because he has cared for us. So we want to give back. Our hope is that those we help will soon be in a position to help others. That is the ultimate goal and the ultimate success because helping others is the ultimate blessing.

AFTERWORD

He was arguably the greatest professional athlete in American history. A poll of top sports journalists would undoubtedly place him unanimously in the top five. He was on the covers of *Newsweek, Sports Illustrated,* and *Time* in the same week—a feat accomplished by no other athlete. He was described in *Time* as having "a neck like a buffalo, a back as broad as a sofa."

Pete Axthelm of *Newsweek* wrote, "He is a banner of health and rippling power," claiming that watching him leaves observers "convinced that, for one of those moments that seldom occur in any sport, they have witnessed genuine greatness."

I don't have anything that would qualify as a "man-cave." But I do have three pictures of Secretariat on my basement wall. Only one of them bears the autograph of Ron Turcotte, the jockey associated with the racing sensation also known as "Big Red," and "America's Super Horse." And they are not framed audaciously, so as to leave visitors in awe. They are there for my appreciation alone.

Secretariat was born on March 30, 1970, at The Meadow Stud in Doswell, Virginia, to parents, Somethingroyal and Bold Ruler. Who better to produce an offspring that would wear the crown of American horse racing?

At age three, Secretariat became the first horse to win the Triple Crown in a quarter of a century. By then he was already widely celebrated—he'd been the first two-year-old to be named Horse of the Year. He would, of course, become the first horse to enjoy that title in back-to-back years.

By the time Secretariat stepped onto the dirt track at Belmont in 1973, the first two legs of the Triple Crown were already his, and he had sixteen wins, three track records, and two world records to his credit. Most speedy horses entering the Belmont Stakes with a chance at Triple Crown glory fade in the last quarter-mile of the grueling one-and-a-half-mile race. So the question was: would he last? It wasn't a question the odds makers took too seriously. Secretariat entered the race as a ten-to-one favorite.

Halfway through the race, Secretariat was neck and neck with Sham, the only horse to challenge him in the Kentucky Derby and the Preakness. But Sham spent himself trying to keep up and began to fade.

Secretariat did the opposite, pouring on the speed and extending his lead to fifteen links, then eighteen, twenty-one, twenty-five, and finally winning by thirty-one lengths. He set a world record and shattered the track record by two and three-fifths seconds.

More than forty years later, no winner of the Belmont has yet posted a time within two seconds of Secretariat's two minutes and twenty-four seconds. He would go on to finish his amazing career with a six-and-a-half-length win on the one-and-five-eighths-mile track at the Canadian International Championship Stakes.

Secretariat has always inspired me. He set high standards that created high expectations and consistently rose to the occasion by outperforming the bar he had set.

The members of his support team equally inspired me. They made it possible for Secretariat to have his opportunity to shine and for fans of horse racing around the world to experience the thrill of watching America's Super Horse.

Great expense (and risk), time, patience, nurturing, and coordinated care by owners, trainers, groomers, exercise riders, veterinarians, and many others led to the race-day finishing touches of Secretariat's jockey, Ron Turcotte. Everyone did his or her part. If they hadn't, no one would have ever heard the name Secretariat.

Similarly, I am inspired to look back and recall the contributors that made it possible for the name REG to carry historical significance in the growing renewable energy industry. Every piece of a complicated puzzle had to come together and fit just right or we would have never gotten out of the gate.

From a personal standpoint, my parents and family gave me an irreplaceable foundation of love, character, work ethic, and faith—pillars that could support the construction of a good life and significant accomplishments.

My sons, Greg, Mike, and Matt, have supplied an abundant incentive and joy across the years of my adult life. And from the time of our marriage in my latter days at Purina to present, my wife Terry has been my delight and an invaluable "can-do" support system. I would have never made it through all the ups and downs, challenges, and disappointments, without her unwearied encouragement.

Ralston Purina gave me the job right out of college that became a thirty-three-year career and offered a wealth of experience, particularly in the area of risk management, which would prove critical to everything that followed in my life. Superiors—like Ed Cordes, Jim Hogan, and others—mentored me, directed my training, and managed my development all the way to Purina's executive suite in St. Louis.

And countless colleagues from the science labs to the floor of the Chicago Board of Trade contributed to team accomplishments that not only made me proud but eager to get to work every day.

Doug Stidham, Jeff Stroburg, and the board at West Central gave me a shot when no one else would. They and others repeatedly supported my ideas with their confidence on numerous fronts, including that of making a comeback after the plant explosion—an expensive comeback at that.

Without Myron Danzer, biodiesel production at West Central would have been a brief conversation about an intriguing concept. Without his ingenuity and determination, dozens of my other ideas would have been untenable. The word "quit" does not exist in Myron's dictionary.

Like Myron, Dan Oh, Brad Albin, Dave Elsenbast, Jason Schwennecker, Paul Nees, Jon Scharingson, Matt Schultes, Gary Haer, and countless others had key roles in REG's success.

When our biodiesel vision eclipsed West Central's ability to commit to biodiesel, the company continued as a foundational investor. It was a starting point for going out and getting international players like ED&F Man and Bunge to back REG financially. Having those two well-known giants of the agriculture industry behind us was of great value in another way: name-dropping clout. Their association ensured that we got at least a hearing with Goldman Sachs, Morgan Stanley, UBS, and others, which led important investors NGP Energy Technology Partners and Natural Gas Partners to also take a risk on REG.

It wasn't just pieces fitting together, but the right pieces right on time. But did right on time mean fitting together the first time?

Absolutely not!

Success required persistence, tenacity, lots of hard work, and dedication to excellence. It also took plenty of prayer and faith.

More than once, my experience was like that of Ron Turcotte directing Secretariat through a field of competition at breakneck speed. At many decision points along our course, I was flying on instinct, trusting the tools of sound judgment that were in place. I had been trained for this. I believed in what we were doing. And countless times, decisions hinged on unflinching trust in people around me—an important part of the complex of professional instinct.

Of course, my appreciation of Secretariat goes back to my beginnings as a young trainer. I know what it is to train a young horse to be a partner, a team player, a winner. At a height of 16.5 hands and carrying 1,200 pounds of "rippling power," a horse with as much spirit and competitive fire in his belly as Secretariat could easily have been out of control. His trainer, Lucien Laurin, was the one who quietly guided raw material, talent, and personality to the realization of optimal potential. Lucien Laurin never made the cover of *Time, Newsweek,* or *Sports Illustrated* ... or *The New York Times.* Laurin's was a job well done when Secretariat made the headlines.

That is how I have always viewed being an employee (at whatever level). When my efforts contribute a bit of shine to the company marque, a benefit to our customers, and measurable bottom line growth, my work has been rewarded. It's the trainer in me. Yes, I had my ten minutes of fame in *The New York Times* and on the NASDAQ building in Times Square when REG went public. But it was in the quietness of my home in Innsbrook when I saw the name REG in a headline about being chosen by the NFL to power the Super Bowl that I felt most deeply pleased.

The same is true of my life and work in the context of Christian faith. A scriptural instruction puts it this way: "Whatever you do, work at it with all your heart, as working for the Lord ... it is the Lord Christ you are serving" (Col. 3: 23, 24).

That has always been my attitude. When it is all said and done, it pleases me most to see that Jesus, my Lord, is honored.

The Innsbrook stables are a few minutes from our home. There, I have tall stately Appaloosas in two of the stalls: Fancy and Dixi.

Terry and I enjoy going to the stables, caring for the horses, and riding together. But training them is what I really enjoy. In fact, training them fulfilled a lifelong dream of mine: competing on a national level.

My career years were not conducive to anything as time-consuming as work in the ring to prepare for national competition. I was pushing it at times to keep horses as a modest hobby. In fact, when Terry and I moved to Wichita after Koch Industries bought Purina, I didn't have horses for several years.

But in 2003, I stumbled upon a horse farm in Iowa where owner and breeder, Dr. Ken Friday, had some outstanding Appaloosa bloodlines. I purchased a three-year-old filly, Fourwheelin's Dixi Chic.

Not only had I lacked the time to invest in national competition, I lacked the quality of horse necessary to face premium-bred competition. Dixi was of that quality.

I trained Dixi and entered her in a handful of competitions throughout the Midwest in 2004. It is difficult to receive a national point, so I knew coming away with a point or two would be a challenge. But Dixi performed well, receiving five national points.

One of the shows was so populated with great horses that the competition lasted past midnight. When it was all over, Dixi had taken third place in her class. Exiting the arena, I felt a little disappointed to have come so close and only get third place. But I ran into Dr. Ken Friday. Beaming, he said, "Are you aware you just lost to number one and number two in the country?"

"No," I responded. "I had no idea."

Competing with Dixi that year was a great experience, and it left me wanting more. That, plus the fact that two horses were required for Terry and me to ride together, led to my purchasing Dixi's half-sister, Fancy Fourwheelin, in 2006.

We trained Fancy and got her ready to compete in 2007. But her first show was a disaster. She spooked, knocked the pylons over, dragged me a few paces, broke her headstall, and ran for the exit. Her behavior was so out of control that other exhibitors were scared, and I was mortified.

Thankfully, that horrendous start was not Fancy's last competition. We pressed on, showing almost weekly throughout the summer across numerous states.

Rankings are based on national points accumulated during the year. And at the end of the year, Fancy ranked in the top ten nationally in three of the six categories in which we had competed. Once again, through perseverance and consistency, the pieces came together.

This was a great accomplishment because it meant we'd gone up against the pros and had repeatedly come away with national points. But it wasn't just about accumulating points; for me, it was culminating six decades of horse training that began on the Ramsbottom family farm with my first horse, Blondie. Not entering the competitions as a pro, I was as surprised as anyone when Fancy and I came away with those national rankings. The rankings were the capper to the rewards of our relational character.

Recently, Terry and I were working with Fancy and Dixi in a training corral. There was no audience, just us. No points were on the line. I was riding Fancy through some maneuvers requiring a high level of discipline when an unlikely trio of renegades showed up at the open end of the corral. One was a spirited pony that had gotten free. One was a donkey. And one was a fat little black terrier of some sort that looked more like a pot-bellied pig.

The dog was slightly behind the other two and began barking. Thirty yards in the distance, the horse's handler was coming to get it. The pursuit inspired the runaway horse to gallop around the outside of the corral, its two new friends in tow.

Fancy froze, distracted and perhaps jealous. It is, after all, natural for a powerful animal built for speed to want to run freely, especially if others are doing it. Additionally, horses are curious animals. Charging off in some direction to find out what's going on is an ever-active compulsion.

Handling the situation within the context of what we were there to accomplish in the ring together, I talked to Fancy and gently guided her through some familiar commands. This brought her attention back to our routine.

From there, everything went smoothly, reinforcing our relational integrity. Blondie would have been proud. It confirmed what I learned from her many years in the past: relationship matters.

EPILOGUE

At the end of the day, what is the value of the journey? What does experience offer in reflection that is of any benefit?

I believe it all comes down to purpose.

Purpose is what we all care about. Without it, we are left dissatisfied and disappointed, just wandering wherever, doing whatever. Purpose is what we yearn to discover and then fulfill.

Unique to every person, purpose is the key to happiness. God made us that way. It began with Him. He created us to care about His purpose and pursue it with everything we've got to throw at it.

"But I have no idea what God wants me to do," someone might say.

Because purpose began with God, our search has an evident starting point: He cares. He cared about our purpose before we did. He had it in mind when He created us. We have to seek it, but we don't begin seeking purpose blindly.

We begin with this confidence: God cares. The fact is implied—like a fingerprint He left behind—in the burning desire we have to find and live out our purpose. Knowing that He cares, our logical first action is to pray. And like right and left feet taking steps on a long, patient walk in the same direction, prayer and action work together to inform and propel us forward purposefully.

We cannot overstate the importance of taking action, even if the action for the moment is to be still and listen—to God and others we know have our best interest at heart. Listening well is critical because our strong yearning for purpose can easily lead us into dangerous territories of misplaced longing (immorality, addictions, dishonesty, violence, and such).

Of course, we can take many other kinds of actions when our time for listening ends and we've received guidance. And only in the rarest cases will guidance arrive in a flash of light or hand-delivered in a neatly wrapped package with a guarantee attached.

Nevertheless, we must act. No one ever progressed toward purpose without action—usually, the more bold and decisive the better! If the action turns out to be questionable, we can always make corrections and learn lessons. This is all part of the discovery process.

I have found one action to be an especially faithful help in defining purpose: service.

Service begins with compassion. You notice someone else's need and act to remedy it. Some people go all the way to foreign lands to serve others. While those efforts are admirable, they are not a requirement. Just look around, notice who is in need,

Service begins with compassion.

and act! Before you know it, you will find happiness at an all-time high, blessings will be abundant, and purpose will be transformed from a quest to an on-going life achievement.

A PERSONAL REVIEW

My journey may speak to your journey with a helpful insight or two via this book. But it is not your journey. Yours is a unique adventure, and your own words will be much more effective in securing lasting impact from these pages. A simple written review in your own words will aid retention and application of valued content. Here are a few prompts. Jot down your answers to the following questions here, or write or type them. Then write "revisit that book" into your calendar. Next, pull it back off the shelf or put your answers in a self-addressed stamped envelope, and entrust the envelope to a friend who will mail it back to you randomly in a month or two.

1. What is "relational character" and how have your own experiences demonstrated its importance?

2. How is negotiating part of your everyday life?

3. What are the keys to excellence in negotiation?

4. In what ways is preparation the most important factor in successful leadership?

5. What is the makeup of a successful team?

6. What is the nature of true listening?

7. What is transparency and what are its benefits?

8. How do challenging questions serve development of vision and partnerships?

9. Why is celebration important?

10. What is your purpose on your journey?